From Homosexuality To Demon Possession:
A Testimony of Deliverance

Dominique Trumbo

From Homosexuality To Demon Possession:

A Testimony of Deliverance

Dominique Trumbo

Book Cover - Christopher Negron of Negron Design
(Website: www.Negron-Design.com)

Editor - Var Kelly of Just Write It Services (JWIS), LLC
(Email: Info@JustWriteItServices.com |
Website: www.JustWriteItServices.com)

ISBN: 979-8-9918600-1-7

DEDICATION

This book is dedicated to my late maternal grandparents, Rance and Pearl Fondren. You two were likened to my best friends during very lonely years when I felt so misunderstood and rejected. Your love and attention helped me get to where I am today. So, I dedicate this book to the two of you.

Rest in Heaven, as I will see you all again!

ACKNOWLEDGMENTS

To Jade Trumbo, my 18-year-old daughter: What helped carry me through every day of incarceration was knowing I would have you to re-begin with, to start over with, to try again with. You make me so very proud. Your name is exactly what you are to me and your mother, LaShonda. Jade, a jewel you are. Your best life is fast approaching, and I will strive to be the very best father and holy example to you. Thank GOD for giving you to me and your mother. I love you more than anybody.

To my Mom and Dad (stepdad) Betty and Marcus Jones: Your unending love, wisdom, ministry, and counsel through the often-turbulent decades of my life have been a huge benefit to me. Not only were you two there for me over and over during my much earlier years, but even now, as I have been transitioning to a more impactful and greater life. I thank you two for your patience with me. You're the best parents anyone could ever hope for.

To my spiritual mother, the Late Bishop Iona E. Locke, D.D. Th.D.: You believed in my ministry when nearly no one else did. You gave me your own pulpit to preach and prophesy in several times. I will never forget you and how you groomed me for excellence in ministry. I miss you deeply. I owe a lot to you.

To my spiritual parents, Bishop Michael and Mother Stacey Densmore: I deeply love you two. Thank you for being what I needed when Mother Locke transitioned to Glory. Your constant ear and uplifting advice continue to help me reach the goals GOD has given me. Thanks for never leaving my side.

To my spiritual Daughter, Chatan: GOD used you greatly to bring this book to pass. Without your help, this book would not have been made possible. May the blessing of The Lord 'that maketh rich and with it addeth no sorrow' bless you beyond measure until you are filled with wealth.

To another spiritual Daughter of mine, Patricia Vann: You told me years ago to write a book, but I was too busy and chose not to. Then I went to prison, and after I got free on the inside, you told me again. And here the book is now. Thank you, daughter.

To The Ecclesia, the School of Prophets I formed in 2017: You all are nothing less than my family. I love and appreciate each of you.

To Dr. Var Kelly, the owner of Just Write It Services: You helped me self-publish this book and edit it to where I desired it to be. It's apparent your skills are beyond the normal. Aside from your extreme editing capability and professionalism, you are very patient, very humble, and kind. I thank you, Dr. Kelly. I highly recommend you. (www.JustWriteItServices.com)

TABLE OF CONTENTS

INTRODUCTION

You are about to embark on a journey that reveals the darkest depths of spiritual warfare—one that takes you into the enemy's camp and, by GOD's grace, leads you out of it. This book is not just my story; it's a testimony of the relentless battle between good and evil that every single one of us faces, whether we realize it or not. The enemy, Satan, has a plan, and he will use any method, any vice, and any weakness to drag us into his world of bondage and possession. For me, that method was homosexuality. But make no mistake—the enemy isn't concerned with what your vice is. His goal is the same for all of us: to take us away from GOD and into his own dominion of demonic control.

My story is one of being lured into a world of darkness, a world I didn't even fully understand until I found myself deeply entangled, and possessed by demons that sought to destroy me from the inside out. The pain, the shame, the confusion—it all seemed impossible to escape. But as you'll see, GOD was always there, offering deliverance, offering freedom, even when I couldn't see the way out.

This book isn't just for those who have battled with

1

homosexuality. It's for anyone who feels trapped, bound, and oppressed by any form of sin or spiritual attack. Maybe for you, it's an addiction. Maybe it's bitterness, anger, pride, or fear. The enemy doesn't discriminate—he will use whatever door you leave open in order to enter your life. But let me tell you this: no matter how far the enemy drags you, GOD's power to deliver is greater. GOD's love reaches beyond the strongest chains that bind you, and His grace is sufficient to pull you out of the deepest pit.

As you read, I challenge you to look deeper into your own life. What doors have you left open? What battles are you fighting that seem too strong to win? Know this—GOD's desire is for you to be free. The methods of Satan are deceptive, and they can feel overwhelming. But GOD's methods are redemptive and will always lead you to freedom.

This is a story of deliverance. It's a call to recognize the enemy's tactics and seek GOD's freedom with all your heart. My prayer for you is that as you read each page, you will see that no matter how dark things may seem or what vice or struggle has its hold on you, deliverance is not only possible—it's GOD's promise.

Read this book because you need the freedom it reveals. Read this book so you can know the tactics of the enemy. Read this book so you can overcome.

Satan has plans, but GOD has better ones. And this book is your invitation to discover what those plans are.

May each page lead you closer to The One who sets the captives free!

CHAPTER 1
THE DEVIL'S DOORWAY

Satan Wants What GOD Wants

I was born in 1974. I have three siblings: two younger sisters and an older brother.

In some ways, my family life as a child was the usual. There were games, family, fun, and quarrels. My brother and I would run through the house as toddlers, playing with one another. As an older child, I would often fight with my sisters. These were typical interactions between my brother and sisters during our young ages.

When I was in elementary school, my mother divorced our father. He had some outstanding mental health challenges that often caused him to be absent, and when he was there, things often went wrong in the house.

I do not recall a lot about my early childhood. I do have some memories from kindergarten, elementary school, and beyond, but those memories are scattered and far between. Many of the memories I recall probably aren't what you want to remember. You will read about some of them in the chapters of this book.

But The Lord had a plan despite the enemy's strategy.

Around the age of four, I had my first encounter with the divine, with the supernatural. This encounter occurred before I started kindergarten. We had a two-bedroom apartment, and I remember seeing an angel of GOD standing in that apartment's bathroom in the Hollow Creek subdivision of Lexington, Kentucky. What led to the encounter was fear of the dark. The light bulb in the bathroom was out, and I woke up early one morning needing to urinate.

The night before this encounter, I slept in the room with my mom. That morning, I awoke and began to piss on the wall because, like I said, the bathroom light was out. My mother soon awakened and told me to go to the bathroom. After entering that dark room, I saw a tall, glowing, and spectacularly bright angel standing before me. The devil and his fallen angels saw this first recalled spiritual encounter of my life. I feel that this awareness of the spiritual realm triggered the enemy to identify who I was to GOD. Thinking back to that morning, who knew GOD would introduce such a spiritual environment to me at such an early age?

It was after this divine encounter that the enemy launched his attack. In that same room where I pissed on the wall, next to "the angel's bathroom," I slept on the floor next to my mother, who slept in the bed. And one early morning, I began to fondle myself, and my mother woke up, looked down, and ordered me to stop; she saw my erection through the underwear. This incident occurred approximately the same time frame that I saw the angel in the bathroom. I recall that I saw the angel first and

4

then moved toward masturbation afterward. Satan wants what GOD wants.

It is obvious that many people believe it is very normal for their children to "get to know their own bodies." Some often purposely look past fondling and things of that nature as if it should be normal. Some may very ignorantly encourage such perversion. However, none of it should be overlooked— ever because their body is not their own in the first place.

If you see this in a child, it should be talked about, and the child, male or female, should be encouraged to never engage in masturbation or anything heading towards it. The wise parent will pray against more activity in that area for that child. Prayer can easily block the devil's plans.

I was ordered by my mother to stop, and even though I developed an affection for "self-touch" in the years to come, still, a responsible parent would not ignore such actions. It is a door from the devil into a child's life.

Kissing, Rubbing, And Exploring

A church member's baby was at our apartment when I was around six years of age myself. By then, we had moved from Hollow Creek to Laredo Drive, which was in a different part of town. I was a child myself at the time, but I did something that, thinking back now, was so strange. I kissed this male baby on the lips as he lay in the bed.

Another time, I was riding in Lexington in the backseat of a car. I was about seven years old, and a girl from the church, possibly three years younger than me, sat beside me in the car. I remember putting my hand under her skirt. And I rubbed her panties. At approximately that same time, I was riding in the car again, in the same back seat, with a female, maybe two years younger. And I put my hand under her skirt and pinched her. Maybe I chose a small baby boy and then girls younger than me because I sought control, and each was more defenseless compared to myself at that time.

It seems these car incidents with them happened more than once, though I'm uncertain. The only reaction I recall from either of them was them just quietly watching me violate them. No shock, just watching, like it may have happened to them before. I do not know whether they ever told their parents. We never spoke about it, even years later when I saw them. I don't even know if they remembered.

As I think back, it's obvious that this behavior was taught to me. I was taught these actions by someone(s) at an even younger age, likely when I was a baby myself, and there I was doing the same things that were likely done to me.

In *Jeremiah 1:5*, The Word teaches that GOD knows us even before conception. Not only that, but it also teaches that our purpose was established before our creation. So, the devil, I am confident, knows this because he can spiritually see establishments in the spirit realm. He, like GOD, is also spirit. And you and I were in spirit form before we were given a body. Consequently, the devil engineers and puts into action whatever he can to prevent and often pervert the purpose of GOD in our lives.

As an adolescent, I recall another incident while my mother was driving from Lexington, Kentucky, to Nashville, Tennessee, for a regional meeting that our home church was part of. I was so small back then that I could fit on the floor of the back seat of my mother's car. A teenage girl from the church and her boyfriend rode in the back seat as I sat on the floor. And I was upset with him, as he paid more attention to his girlfriend than to me. I do not know where this originated. But I was so young then. I didn't expect either of them to know why I was mad. But I was visibly angry.

Surely, something had to have happened to me years before as a baby. Something had to have occurred where I had the unnatural attention of a male, and now I no longer had it, but I wanted it. Or maybe something happened to me where, with good intentions, I desired attention from a male, and they did something that made me think this was the right attention to receive from the same sex.

I realize now that I enjoyed going somewhere where I didn't have siblings to compete with for my loving mom's attention. Thus, I recall several incidents during my adolescent days when I did some things that should have never happened. These incidents occurred when I was away from home.

I recall spending much time with my GODparents and their family in North Carolina. They had a son who resembled me in color, and I was attracted to him. As we lay in bed together–due to limited space–I remember him being maybe seven years older. As he slept with his back to me, I would lightly touch his back with affection, though he had no idea—to my knowledge.

7

I also spent time at an aunt's house, as I would occasionally. One of her sons lived there too—he was seven years older than me. Oddly enough, I attempted to give him a back massage one night though he made it clear to me that he was not interested. During that incident, his rejection of my advances caused me to be very embarrassed that he did not accept my flirting.

Spending so much time at my aunt's house, sometimes, I would go into her closet and try on her church hats. She had lots of them, unique and very fashionable. One day, she recognized I had gone through the hats since they were out of order. I don't suppose she ever knew I tried some on. Also, a great aunt, whom I stayed with too, I would do the same thing at her home. I would look through her hats and try them on too.

In this now 21st century, one would say I was questioning my gender identity back then. I obviously wanted to be something else or at least try it out.

Where these desires, explorations, and physical needs developed are unknown to me. Nonetheless, there was a growing void within me during all of those years that I eventually sought to fill with affection and close contact with the same sex. These were questions I didn't speak out loud, or maybe I couldn't put them together into questions then, but I was asking nonetheless through many actions that people mostly never heard or responded to back then.

Nakedness And Fondling

By elementary school, I began to show signs of femininity. These were signs that led my mother to seek my female childhood pastor to start having regular meetings with me, whether at her home or at McDonald's. These meetings were to cause me to know that I was "different" and to pray that GOD would help me to change. These meetings with the pastor were temporarily helpful, I do believe. But I was eventually much too interested and intrigued in other males to care what she had to say. Consequently, and ultimately, I went in a very perverted and homosexual direction.

In the third or fourth grade, I had crushes on girls of various races in my classes, even my pastor's granddaughter, who was my first girlfriend. At this time, I was also manifesting additional feminine tendencies, ones that would last for decades, causing people to conclude that I was gay, whether they knew I was or not.

I had a male friend in elementary school who happened to be non-black. One evening at his home, we watched television on a weeknight while his parents were out. Suddenly, he stood up and undressed himself without warning. Nothing sexual happened between him and me that night or ever. He did not portray feminine characteristics. Still, he got fully naked one evening in front of me. I was shocked, but I did not hurry out of the house. I also don't recall getting aroused, neither was he. Still, I observed his nudity, confused, trying to figure out what was happening. As a child myself, I had made physical contact with children, as I talked about. But to see a friend naked was beyond what I

9

expected, so I was in disbelief and bewildered. I don't recall if our friendship continued after that incident.

Then, there was another kid whose mother was friends with my mother. He and I were in the third or fourth grade at the time. His family lived in a house not very far from our apartment. His father was in the military, and they were there temporarily renting a furnished home while his dad was in town for work in the service. One night, while he and I were lying in bed when I was about ten, we watched Michael Jackson's "Thriller" with his father in the room, sitting in a chair nearby. The room was dark when the boy put his hand under the blanket and began to fondle me. I did not stop him, just like I didn't stop the non-black kid. I was confused about what this meant and why it was happening to me, but I think I enjoyed it this time. And either his father did not see us, or he ignored it. It seems he ignored it. These are two sexually related encounters grafted into my memory, the first two where I was the victim, that I can remember anyway. These occurrences were seeds sown into my soul, and immoral feelings began to unravel even the more.

Gender Identity And Confusion

When the devil knows GOD has called you, he then seeks to prevent your pursuit of GOD and GOD's identity, call, and purpose for you.

We live in a day and age now where we often hear two words: "gender identity." To sum this up, ultimately, it boils down to GOD having created you. The all-knowing and infinite mind of GOD created you and me one way. One way He created you,

10

only one, just one. Male or female. And the devil came to pollute what GOD made you - to introduce us to a lie – to deceive you, me and everyone he can.

'Deception' says we are weak and not strong, that we are sick and not healed, that we are meant to be poor and not wealthy, that we are male and not female and vice versa, that you are physically attracted to a female when they have breasts and sexual organs just like you do. Even if one never changes their physical sex through medical procedures, to have sex with the same gender is still living the same lie, the same deception.

Satan is a deceiver. Satan sought to undo the will of GOD in my life, to cause me to identify myself through his own lens. He sought to intertwine me with his identity and wicked options. What we call "my (own) truth," which is actually the devil's truth for me, is actually a lie. The enemy chose to make me content with various pleasures, pleasures that I could not soon escape.

Pleasures come through encounters that remain in our thoughts long after we engage in those actions. Those pleasures give us the idea and impure conclusion that we are something else— something else other than the man or woman that GOD created us to be. And the devil does not start late. He plans and implements his intentions very early, as he did to me.

In the years following that Hollow Creek angelic encounter, the devil would also visit my sleep with paralysis, often intending to instill fear within me. He wanted me to have fear of him - fear of the dark. He wanted to give me the impression that he had more power than GOD.

11

Why would The Almighty GOD allow all of this for the child that I was? I can't answer that with any of my own understanding. Many children around the world have and do often encounter many terrifying and horrifying situations, even to the point of their own death. But I have to trust that GOD knows best and that He is seeking, even early on, to mature me, to mature you, to mature us. We have to trust GOD.

The fact that you and I lived to tell the story is a testimony that GOD knew what He was doing. He knew what He was doing then and still He does, right now.

CHAPTER 2
GROWING IN CHURCH, STRUGGLING

I Learned To Play Church

So, where did religion come into play in all of this? Where were my Sunday school lessons and all of those long church services during all of these invitations into the devil's pleasures?

I grew up in a very religious and strict home. For as long as I can remember, we were Pentecostal-Apostolic. Rules laid down were rules that were followed with diligent obedience. My sisters only wore skirts and dresses. In the winter, they wore leg warmers under their skirts to school. They also weren't allowed to wear earrings or makeup. We didn't believe in alcohol, smoking cigarettes, or going to the cinema. We did not go to bars either. Another apostolic church in the same city didn't even allow their congregants to attend basketball games. Additionally, at their church, the adults who dated had to have chaperones accompany them during outings. Much of this was religious control instituted by men and not scripture.

Sundays at church began around 10:00 a.m. and typically ended around 10 p.m. This included breaks in between services.

Wednesday night services were for prayer; we normally prayed for about an hour. Friday nights were similar to Wednesday nights except instead with seemingly never-ending Bible study. We learned to be very religious in our actions, and church services were like a stage show to act and air it all on. But some of them learned to practice their walk with GOD daily.

I watched my mother at home cry out to GOD for her children. My stepfather spent many hours studying The Bible and praying at home. Having divorced my father, she married my step dad when I was in the 5th grade. However, what I saw of them did not become a part of me. I did not follow their two GODly examples.

One thing I did as a kid was draw churches and play church. I used to play church with books on the apartment floor to represent the sanctuary. I used coins as the people. I would fill the book covers with pennies (the congregants), and the quarter (bishop) was me. The nickels and dimes were ministers, elders, and musicians. I would even play church in my head, with huge audiences praising before The Lord. Playing church was what I liked to do.

I eventually learned to play what I would not live and make my own way of life. I learned to have a form of GODliness *(2 Timothy 3:5)*, with no will to live a repentant life. Hence, demon possession happened to me decades later.

I Received The Holy Spirit!

Responsibility to GOD is avoided and ignored when we spend time with the things of GOD rather than with GOD directly. Doing things like attending church services and revivals and joining the choir but having no close daily relationship with GOD in our own private life is what many of us mostly gave ourselves to.

I spent years getting to know GOD through church services and the like, but not Him personally. I was going to church, but the church's GOD wasn't going home with me. A relationship was required of young Prophet Samuel with GOD, as noted in *1 Samuel 2:18-3:11*, and it is indeed required of us today, too.

I would regularly, during my childhood, attend church convocations, conferences, and large ministry gatherings. That was my routine well into my teens. As I grew older though, my spiritual life was virtually at a standstill. I attended church, but not GOD. I didn't pray to Him or have a personal relationship with Him. I learned through time to have a resemblance of GOD, but His attributes and characteristics were not my personal choice.

Simultaneously, I was very lonely and widely rejected by Winburn Jr. High School classmates, though I was afforded some friendships there. One was with a preacher's son. His father pastored a Methodist or Baptist church on the north side of Lexington. He and I had been good friends for quite some time, maybe more than a year or two. I would visit him at his home, and I got to know his family too. He lived approximately a twenty-minute walk from my home.

One afternoon, as we were at my home alone, he and I were hanging out in the basement. My brother and I shared a room down there. Without warning to him, I attempted to undress him from the pants down; I was quick enough to see his private parts. He was so shocked that it appeared he began to hyperventilate or have an asthma attack.

As I recall, it was four or five years prior that the non-black kid got nude in front of me, and about one or two years prior, that the other kid fondled me in bed as we watched the Thriller music video. I believe I was acting out what had been done to me by those two, even if it took me some five years and gaining a friendship to have the boldness to do so. I also now understand that I was willing to risk my friendship and brotherhood for my own lusts. My lusts tried to win, and that consistent friendship failed. He took off running to and out the front door. The friendship was over.

Reflecting on how this homosexual spirit perpetuated during my junior high school years, events with young boys continued from my early to mid-teens, 6th through 9th grade, and thereafter. I desired to satisfy and attend to these feelings, no matter what it cost me then and would ultimately cost me decades later.

I remember a tall, feminine-acting guy living in the Winburn subdivision. I don't recall if he went to church. At least I didn't know he did. But I hung out with him at his home before. Nothing sexual happened between us, though. There was also a guy who was maybe ten years older than me, who seemed to have a very slight form of mental illness–he just seemed oddly disconnected at times–and he was also heavily involved with a Pentecostal type of church. He and I made out at least once on the ground outside one night next to my junior high school. I just wanted to be around guys who were like me - non-masculine guys. As I became increasingly feminine acting, it seemed that only guys who acted the same as me would be willing to be around me long.

As perverted as I was speedily becoming, it was in the late 1980s, around the age of 15, when I longed to be filled with The Holy Spirit. I wanted to experience GOD. The Holy Spirit, evidenced by speaking in tongues, was highly sought after, especially in my church and Pentecostal and Apostolic churches in many parts of the United States at that time.

Back then, and in some cases now, to be apostolic was to ultimately believe that being saved was being water baptized in Jesus' Name, as stated in *Acts 2:38*. Also, it meant receiving the gift of The Holy Ghost/Spirit relative to the verses of *Acts 2:1-4*. Thus, reaching the point of water baptism and speaking in tongues was like a milestone in the church I grew up in. It meant, to them and to me back then, that we were finally saved. It further meant you were allowed to go to heaven. Also, my concept of GOD back then was that he was some controlling, heavy-handed, spiteful, and quick-to-anger; a hot-tempered judge who sat on a throne, lacking much or any loving-kindness. While my concept was heavily twisted, my desire was still fulfilled on Saturday, June 2, 1990. I was finally Spirit baptized at Greater

Soul Deliverance Tabernacle in Lexington, KY. I responded to the altar call during that Saturday night revival service, where the now late Evangelist Iona Locke was the guest preacher.

That night, speaking in tongues for me happened almost effortlessly. It was as if that night was waiting for me to go to that altar to receive the Baptism of The Holy Spirit/Ghost. The thing about this experience is that I had already, for years prior, opened my mind, body, and soul to homosexual desires and actions. So, what happened in June of 1990 should have been an escape from all of that because it was GOD taking up residency inside of me. He began to live inside of me. However, a war was on the rise because evil had also found a home inside me years before. This war would one day cause a tremendous explosion.

I do not recall a "honeymoon" with The Lord. This "honeymoon" experience is what many Believers experience after first being baptized with The Holy Spirit. It's like a short-lived high-spirited experience of a very extraordinary relationship with GOD. It causes newly born-again people to experience victory, defeat the desires of their wicked hearts, and conquer that sinful nature. However, there should not be a "honeymoon." We ought to have this experience every day of our lives moving forward with The Holy Ghost. Still, this honeymoon is what many Believers even now, experience short term. As for me, instead of having this experience, a war broke out within me. It was The Holy Spirit vs. Satan. It was the devil's goal to keep me fettered in my worldly lusts, focused on my desires, and tangled in homosexuality.

This was the summer of 1990, and I was at the high hormone age of 16, with no school to attend for weeks—only work at McDonald's. So, even though I had been baptized with The Holy Spirit, there was still a fight, and the devil intended to win. So, he planted more people in my life.

Around this time, a preacher's son from a different state liked me a lot. So, instead of falling in love with GOD, I learned to go to church while falling in "love" with a guy. He was about three or four years my senior.

Seeds Becoming Deeds

I learned a pattern that would coexist with me for decades. This pattern gave me the option (or so I thought) to have what was on the outside, a walk with GOD, which people got to see. But on the inside, a strong and ever-growing lust for the same sex was stirring and further developing.

The devil knows how to pique people's interest in us, causing them to be infatuated with us. His purpose is to keep you and me distracted from GOD. He wants us to focus on those people, relationships, and distractions. Hence, my experience with the preacher's son was such. He pursued me, and I engaged him, but soon, I was very distracted by him.

Back then, we had calling cards to call people long distance. So, I contacted him using calling cards to keep the calls private from my family. I would walk to the neighborhood convenience store to use the phone booth. There, I would be talking flirtatiously to him for long periods of time. These lengthy calls kept me focused on him and not The Holy Ghost. I also recall that he was unattractive, which is likely why he was even more intrigued to be in a relationship with me.

My first climax was with him. I did not know what had happened, but we were in the stairwell of a hotel in Louisville, KY, for a national church event. Anyone could have walked into what we were doing at any time, but sin is stupid, and it makes us stupid. There in the stairwell, we, with our clothes on, were grinding on one another, and without warning, I began to climax in my clothes. I don't recall enjoying it. I was likely too stunned to enjoy it. I had no idea what was even happening.

The preacher's son was around age 19, and I was still a minor of about 16 years. So, we both were young and stupid. However, one thing I realized about him was that he never acknowledged me in public. I sometimes wondered why he didn't acknowledge me around others. I think he kept us a secret because I was so feminine. Though he was feminine, too. But it's evident now that he didn't want people to think we were even friends.

Eventually, after I became unhappy with him, I turned against him. I grew tired of a long-distance relationship, him living approximately a 3-hour drive away. So, I soon lied to him to get out of the relationship. I told him I would expose our relationship to his preacher/father. At that time, this preacher's son already had some health challenges, and this threat from me caused him further issues with his health, likely due to anxiety. So, he soon told me that he had told his father about us for fear that I would, and he never spoke to me again.

This door/relationship and countless others were doors that led to other interactions, and what was inside those doors—those relationships—never satisfied me permanently. It couldn't and never would. Only GOD can genuinely and perpetually satisfy. These doorways were encounters and experiences that further trapped me inside those rooms for many years. Just because I was no longer with the preacher's son didn't mean I wasn't still with a spirit. He was gone, but the spirit that introduced him and had been with me for many years was still present. In fact, he had no plans of leaving. He was preparing to bring other spirits into my life to join him and me.

The devil comes to kill, steal, and destroy *(John 10:10)*. He is a very patient enemy. Demons, like GOD, operate in the spirit realm where there is no time, so demons have a tendency to be very, very patient. All the while, this spirit that had me sexually touching myself as a child and touching others, these demons were planting seeds into my mind and life.

Seeds (e.g., thoughts) can get inside of us and easily become deeds. Meaning that seeds can grow into actions. The enemy watches us closely to determine what we like and even what/who he can attract to us. He uses this information gathered through watching and learning our ways to his advantage in order to trap us more. As these seeds are planted, they grow if not stopped earlier. What was a thought not only became an action but also an action over and over again: deeds.

GOD's Agenda Vs. Satan's Agenda

GOD has an agenda for each of us, and so does the devil. He never stops, he never quits, he never gives up. The devil is intent on wrecking our lives. And he often and very normally has some of us operating in our feelings. What we like, what turns us on, what is appealing and attractive to us. But GOD has the power to keep us in Him, to keep our minds on Him, and to focus us on His will.

Satan has existed for centuries and maybe beyond. His skill, knowledge, and understanding of humanity evolved from the Garden of Eden. So, it's obvious that we need the power of GOD in order to empower us to overcome the devil's expertise, genius, brilliantly formed tests, and unending tactics. You and I can either become an instrument of GOD or the same for the devil. The enemy seeks to fill our lives and schedules with his thoughts, ideas, plans, associates, friendships, marriage(s), practices, future, career, business opportunities, exploits, and academic plans. All of which ultimately lead to a spiritual death unless and until we repent.

He that hath begun a good work in you shall perform/complete it *(Philippians 1:6)*. We need to comply with GOD and do so now. You can choose to do it now or later. But the longer it takes, while you decide to obey Him or not, you also waste precious time. GOD can use any and everything we have been through or chose—even wrong choices—to our ultimate advantage. But every lesson may not have originated with GOD and be necessary to His initial plan for our lives. So, the sooner we learn and submit to GOD, the better off we are.

Threatened With A Knife And Getting Crabs From A Teacher

From the age of 15 to 17, I was employed by McDonald's as a cashier and I performed other duties. After work, I would take a bus home. Once, I recall standing on a corner downtown waiting for a bus when a car pulled up. A man who was about 30 years old, driving a two-door vehicle, pulled up to offer me a ride. I had seen him at a church before. And that was a ride further into homosexual deeds.

This man was an elder in a local church in Lexington, KY. He was brown-skinned and attractive. He lived alone on the western side of town. From that first offer forward, I began to see him as a refuge, a place I could go to during this young homosexual life I was trying to navigate through.

I would often go to see him after school or work. His home allowed me to "feel" loved, accepted, and desired. What I learned from him was intimacy from a man. This taught me to believe that he cared for me. I learned a man could show me the affection I, as a child, sought through the aforementioned others.

Same-sex was actually not often the focus with him, because the devil wanted to make me think he loved me. This relationship was mostly about spending quality time with this church elder, getting to know him, and being around him. It was more than a "relationship." It was friendship with sometimes sexual and intimate benefits from time to time. This friendship taught me that our desires are formed through what we experience with others, too. From this friendship, I learned to seek that same

23

connection with others, where sex was not the main object, but rather companionship, openness, and friendship.

As I got to know this church elder, that lust was and never would be fully content or satisfied. That lust growing inside of me sought to control my whole life and schedule. So, when I wasn't with this elder after work, I stood in front of a gay club in downtown Lexington. I ignorantly stood there to get a ride and to be a hooker with adult strangers; I just wasn't paid. All while I was a minor.

The guys during those promiscuous years ranged from and to various ethnicities, from older to younger, from tall to short, from shaven to bearded. Sin often has no preference. It just wants to keep you busy.

Once, I was picked up by a scruffy, very average-looking, short guy with a go-tee. He was driving a dark red pickup truck. We headed to an apartment complex parking lot not far from downtown, where he expected me to perform pleasure on him right there in the lot. I wasn't thrilled with the idea, and his lack of hygiene and cleanliness caused me to hesitate and refrain. Truthfully, I wanted someone passionate and intimate, like the church elder. The elder was clean, affectionate, and handsome. But this guy just wanted my performance. He was selfish. And when I acted like I would not comply, he drove me to a shopping center on Winchester Rd., where he parked behind it. By then, I had taken off my shoes in the truck's cab to be more comfortable. He then opened the glove compartment and showed me a knife. Then, without a second thought, I jumped–shoeless–out of the truck. So then he pulled off, and I ended up inside of a Wendy's lobby. I used their phone and called the church elder. He came and picked me up and then dropped me off near my home.

The church elder later told me that he drove around town that night, looking for the guy. He told me he was very angry at what the pickup truck driver had done to me. So he sought some sort of revenge. Thankfully, he never found him. This incident caused me to identify him as a protector. He was very apparently not interested in stopping my life from heading in that direction, but he certainly wanted to keep me from harm. However, real love would not seek to continue to receive sexual contact from me–a minor and male like him–while seeking to protect me. He was a predator and even a pedophile. His motive was selfish. He never loved me. It was pure lust.

My mother, who, to me, has the gift of the word of knowledge. She was home praying one night, and I came into the foyer from outside. She was crying out to GOD for me, and her other children, as she often did. That particular night, she told me that The Lord had shown her a vision of me getting out of a white car. Little did she naturally know that that is exactly what color car the church elder drove and that I had just gotten out of his car moments before walking up the street home.

Parents ought to be prayerful and sensitive enough to think not only about what their child might be doing. But to know and see it through prayer and then to pray against it.

During that season of my life, I longed to be in the presence of gay men. It was so consuming that I would even attend HIV meetings, where there were all or mostly only white men present.

Though no sexual flings resulted from these meetings. I still wanted to be near them.

In some way or another, I would regularly meet up with and have sexual interactions with men in Lexington. There were a string of them during this time in my life. I once had a sexual interaction with a thirty-ish guy–he was more into himself than me as often same sex encounters are. This guy was part of a gospel choir. I recall another interaction with a schoolmate in Lexington's Festival Market's bathroom. Eventually, we met up at his home when his mom was away. Then, there was another guy. He had a sports car at my school–Lafayette High School–and would sometimes give me a ride. He declined my pursuit to be sexual with him. My teen years were very filled with either failed attempts or successful ones at some sort of sexual interaction with either men or guys around my own age.

Another encounter I cannot forget. This man was a male teacher from Winburn who had since retired. He lived in a high-rise building in downtown Lexington. I went to his downtown apartment one day and had a sexual interaction with him. I was about 16, and I–very apparently–had contracted crabs from him. After going to his place, I recall itching and itching in my groin. At some point, confessing it to my mother, she directed my brother to take me to the hospital. They soon determined it was crabs, as there were tiny spots of blood all over my underwear in the crotch area. I got a product called "Rid." But I soon determined that the only way to eliminate these body lice was to cut off my pubic hair, so I did. That crab episode ended - until years later, when I was married.

One account during this time in my life that stands out is with a female at McDonald's. She suddenly kissed me at work one day. We were on break. Though I was uninterested in her. I yearned for what I felt like with the church elder. That lustful spirit had already locked its grip on me so much that even a passionate kiss from a female didn't entice me. But I came to understand soon that the church elder was also intimate with other men or underage boys, which is likely why I sought other sexual opportunities because I could not have all of him.

All of this, over and over, man after man, attempt after attempt, occasion after occasion after occasion, time after time, was me searching, needing, wanting, desiring, further trying to fill a lust. A lust from within. A lust that would eventually seek to kill me, to steal my time, my body, and my walk with GOD.

CHAPTER 3
LOVE, CONFUSION, AND EARLY TRIALS

Starting College And Starting Sex

After being fired from McDonald's–for my bad attitude–at 17 and then quitting Hardee's to work for Baskin Robbins 31 Flavors Ice Cream, I sought to meet men through dating advertisements in the local newspaper. I was still occasionally involved with the church elder, but around 17 or 18, I met a college student from Atlanta. He was just a few years older than me, and he acted masculinely. He was attending college in a nearby city, and he worked in the city.

We sometimes made out in the work storage room after work when I was there alone. We even made out one day as we watched a movie at the theater around the corner from the ice cream shop. The way he looked at me was the same sort of infatuation that the preacher's son had with me. That same look was also in the college student's eyes. He loved me, so I thought.

He rented a small studio-style apartment on Nicholasville Rd, and he and I spent many times together at his apartment, often making out. He had an unusually large nose and a box-style haircut. He was about 5' 9 and around 160 lbs. He even sought anal intercourse. But I couldn't figure out how to accomplish that, so we left that alone. He even helped me to choose the first car I bought—a Ford Thunderbird. I cherished, once again, having someone who wasn't just sexual, but also friendship. This caused me to believe that he actually did love me. Yet, I later understood that this college student wanted commitment. He wanted committed love in return, and I wasn't ready for commitment.

By the fall of 1993, I was heading to Louisville, having just graduated from Lafayette High School, to attend RETS Institute of Technology, a computer science and electronics school that was based in Louisville and later closed down. Soon before I left for studies, I began to repent to The Lord. I discontinued my relationship with the college student from Atlanta, deeply hurting him. He was my first boyfriend. He was also the first to be willing to hang with me in public.

In October 1993, I left for RETS, an approximate 1-hour drive from Lexington. By then, I was walking the straight and narrow path of obedience to GOD. However, it did not last long. Weeks after my moving into an apartment that I shared off school property with three other male RETS students, they invited me to go to a titty bar with them. The shirtless woman served us. That night, I experienced alcohol for the very first time. I literally drank a 6-pack of beer in about one hour. That same night, I also vomited onto the floor at the entrance of our door to the apartment.

I recall deciding to go home for Thanksgiving that fall. As I was driving back to Louisville, I planned to go out to party at a primarily white-attended club in downtown Louisville. But the car broke down on the highway. Thankfully, a kind person gave me a ride to Louisville, and that night, being nineteen, I entered a gay club for the very first time. And the devil had already invited someone there to take up more of my time, just as he had put me there.

I stood on the edge of the dance floor, and there, in the dark, was a tall Caucasian guy with blond hair who looked very handsome—in the dark—reminding me of the well-known actor and model—at least in the dark. A relationship transpired between me and the tall white male. Though there was little to no intimacy between him and I. He was more of a companion and friend than anything else. But his home was still a place I could go and hang out. He lived in the west end of Louisville and he had a high interest in young black guys. At some point early on, he did admit to me that he was HIV positive. Men were dying from AIDS at a very alarming rate during that decade of the 1990s, and this relationship occurred 1993-1994.

He seemed often infatuated with me. But I was much too busy checking out the gay scene of Louisville, often attending on weekends either at the white club or a mostly black-attended "hole in the wall" club, also located in downtown Louisville. I made friends like "Jason," who began to wear women's clothes—drag. Jason was a very beautiful mixture of black, white, and Latino. He and I also hung out with "David," and all of us were approximately the same age.

31

By about the summer of 1994, I met "Tyrone" at the black club. He was about 6 feet, very muscular, very-very handsome, and masculine. It was clear almost immediately that Tyrone was not infatuated with me in the least. Rather, he was very self-centered. And I was naive enough to fall into his trap.

It was the first night that I met him when we spent it together in his unkempt upper bedroom. And for the first time I engaged in completed sex with a male. He lived in the east end of Louisville on the second level of a home.

Though our romance was short-lived, as I soon learned he was promiscuous. After I learned this I broke up with him.

I did think then that I loved Tyrone. I even cried, having called his mother to tell her he cheated on me. But she seemed to already know that he was a whoremonger.

So I kept going to clubs throughout 1994, but I never had another boyfriend besides Tyrone for many years, at least not anyone I referred to as my boyfriend.

She Prayed for The Family and Me

During that same year of 1994, I was friends with another drag-dresser, this time a white guy, whom I invited over to the apartment. Soon after arriving, he had sexual relations with one of my roommates. When RETS learned I had invited a "drag queen" to the apartment, they put me out of the apartment. I then moved in with the tall white guy whom I met that Thanksgiving weekend of 1993.

Not long after that, I obtained a rented room off Dixie Highway, living on the second floor of a single-family home. I was working staffing service jobs by then. That same year, I tried a cigarette once. I also smoked marijuana a few times. Marajuana and cigarettes were not my lust, men were.

My precious and beloved grandmother Pearl was ill with cancer during the year 1994. As she became more and more ill, I stopped dressing as feminine as I usually had. I would often darken my mustache by this time. I guess a thicker mustache appearance made me feel more manly looking. I previously also carried a purse-like pouch and wore my own nails long, clear, and polished. But as her illness came towards her death, I began wearing more masculine attire, such as boots, baggy jeans, etc. I'm unsure what brought this on other than GOD preparing to shift my life.

By the end of that year, my beloved grandmother Pearl Fondren died of cancer on Wednesday, December 7th, 1994.

Oh, how I loved her so very much. She and my granddaddy Rance were like my best friends during much of my teens and pre-teens. I spent countless hours visiting them during my elementary and middle school years, even staying overnight sometimes. I felt no judgment at their home, as I often experienced at school and church. Sincere love and importance was what I felt from them both, along with more space. The focus was on me when I was there. Since I had three siblings at home it was sometimes hard to get the attention I longed for. I love and miss both of them deeply and dearly: Pastor Elder Rance and my granny Pearl Fondren, my maternal grandparents.

33

I have always believed that my granny prayed on her deathbed that if GOD took her, she would only agree to leave us if he saved me and others in our family. I still believe that to this day. Many of us, their offspring, have been saved since her passing - many.

I Obeyed GOD

It was the night of Friday, January 20, 1995. I attended a church service at Greater Bethel Temple in Louisville, KY, 834 S. 3rd Street. The now late pastor was Suffragan Bishop Eugene Stewart. After the message of a guest speaker, he invited people up for prayer. The Lord drew me there, to the altar. The minister at the altar, Elder Maurice Marshall, could tell I wasn't coming clean with GOD–I wasn't ready to let go of the past.

So Elder Marshall took me to the fellowship hall, telling me I had to confess something. I then remorsefully confessed my sins to the elder, the life I had been living. It was then that The Holy Ghost began to reactivate within me. Right there in that fellowship hall, I began to speak in tongues as The Spirit of GOD gives utterance. Later that night, I went home alone.

The next night, Saturday, I was lonely and returned to a nightclub. Soon disappointed with my irresponsible decision, I repented again and found myself at church the following Sunday Morning.

I attended another rather large apostolic faith church in Louisville, KY; not Greater Bethel Temple. This apostolic church's pastor is now deceased too. Nevertheless, that large apostolic church was soon a wilderness for me, a place of extreme loneliness. I could readily tell that they saw me as different. That difference became more known to me in March of 1995. GOD said to me on a Sunday morning before going to church to tell them during the testimony service that morning that He had delivered me from homosexuality. I obeyed GOD. Their pastor was one of the first to stand up with an ovation, as most of them did, applauding my honesty, I assume. You would then have thought that I would have been greatly loved and embraced by them, but it was the exact opposite.

Eventually, a few young brothers, a couple of older ladies, and three young ladies embraced me somewhat. Yet, the overwhelming majority of the church members, the congregants, mostly ignored me and very obviously distanced themselves from me. At every service, I felt like an outcast, meaningless to them, and unworthy–to them–to be there. But I kept on showing up. I kept going because it was the will of GOD that I do so.

After church services, the various groups and cliques conversed and mingled throughout the sanctuary, but I was left alone. I hated being shunned and forsaken, but I remained faithful there because it was GOD's will. Their rejection hurt me over and over, but I obeyed GOD.

On Mother's Day 1995, GOD also told me to testify at my childhood church in Lexington, KY, that He delivered me from homosexuality. My mother was not there that Sunday; she was at the gravesite of my precious grandmother Pearl, who by then had only been deceased for several months. But I still testified. I obeyed GOD.

About a month later, the now world renowned Bishop Jackie McCullough was in revival at Greater Bethel Temple on 3rd Street. On Friday night of Father's Day weekend, I stood up and obeyed GOD. I gave my testimony. The saints rejoiced. But right after service, a member of the other large apostolic church I had been attending since late January, a male member who was quite effeminate, waited for me on the church steps to congratulate me on my testimony. He was maybe five years older than me.

Shortly afterwards, that night he invited me to his place, and while there was no strong connection between the two of us, we were still intimate with one another. Almost immediately after that, I struggled with my disobedience, and by the next week, I went to see the apostolic church pastor where he and I attended. I told the pastor what I had done and with whom. He looked and seemed disgusted with me. If he wasn't already against me by then, he indeed was now. It was as if he despised my very presence at "his" church. But I stayed faithful there. I obeyed GOD.

This apostolic church had a Sunday school class, where they taught newcomers dress code rules and much of their own laws of salvation. It was taught by a stern and rigid assistant pastor. I graduated from the class, my picture was taken, and I felt so good that I was finally accepted. So, the graduates' photographs were all placed on the wall in the church's vestibule, but my picture was missing. This meant I was still not a member of their church. No matter how faithful I was, I was never accepted, welcomed, or allowed to be a member of their church.

By about 1997, it was The Year of Prayer. Each year, their pastor gave a name, a focus, and an agenda for that year. That year, they had prayer every single morning, and I was there every single morning until I wrecked my car one morning from being so sleepy driving home from 6 am prayer. Faithful or not, I was never accepted as one of them. But I loved GOD, and I wouldn't let Him down. I was still always there.

Although their church refused to accept me, GOD continued to meet me at home. At home, I would pray all night, read the entire Bible cover to cover, and fast for days at a time. GOD would meet me, commune with me, talk to me, and fellowship with me, and I loved every single moment of it. They didn't love me, but He did and He made sure I knew it.

"I Love You."

Eventually, GOD told me to share my testimony with a guy I worked with. I hesitated. I barely knew the guy. Then, The Lord said to me a statement that would live with me forever. It was the initiation of the covenant between He and I. GOD said: "I will make you a great man if you obey My every command." I obeyed GOD, and I shared my testimony with this stranger. Months later, the covenant was confirmed when an arch, a colored rainbow made up of circles in the form of an arch, appeared "on" my bedroom window one day. I understood that it was GOD affirming the covenant, which I wouldn't often keep, but one day, I would learn to heed to it.

Those times at home when not at church or work were very difficult often. And the enemy sought to make me fearful of the dark again, as I was as an adolescent. One particular night, a demon seemingly climbed on my back during my all-night prayer as I prayed in my dark bedroom. The best way I can describe the feeling is like a thick heavy sensational dark electric. Another time, three demons stood at the bottom of the bed as I lay in the dark room; the one in the middle was the tallest. On another occasion, as I prayed fearfully with the light kept on, I fell asleep on my knees on the sofa-type chair, and a spirit of paralysis attacked me. I could suddenly not move. The devil wanted me to be afraid to pray, but it did not work. I may have been fearful, but I still prayed. Despite every attack, GOD enabled me to press.

And GOD is still calling us to press today. In spite of the many trials and tribulations we may face right now – in our individual lives, in our homes, communities – and even in this nation and the world – GOD is still calling us all to pray and lay at His feet. These are the times and the moments when GOD hastens to help, cultivate, and deliver us. We must press, no matter what.

My first encounter with personal deliverance from demons occurred around 1996. I had read a book entitled: "Pigs in the Parlor." That book, which captured national and international attention many years ago, teaches in much detail the power of GOD to deliver and, more importantly, the steps to take in order to be delivered. Once, I adhered to the book's direction and began to rebuke the devil from my body. And unexpectedly, phlegm came out of my throat as I coughed it up. This was my first self-deliverance experience, the first of many deliverances to come.

Still, I struggled to please GOD. One particular night, I got in my vehicle and was heading on the interstate to another area in town to engage in perversion with a male. As I drove the car, GOD spoke to me and said, "I love you." In other words, as you, Dominique, travel this interstate to search for what you think is love, know that you won't find it and that I love already. Those absorbing words, "I love you," brought tears to my eyes. So, I turned the car around and headed back home to sleep alone, but not alone. He loves me, and He loves you too.

The more time I spent with GOD, the more He anointed me. I received a great anointing in worship. My worship was often extreme and unusual. During worship, it was as if GOD Himself would press down on my back, causing me to bow down before Him in worship. And it was clear that the church I had been attending detested it. Watching me reverence GOD seemed to make them sick.

What we identify as worship and praise in the church can be so inside the box and so ordinary, limited, and restrained. Through me, GOD introduced them to worship without boundaries. Sometimes, I would end up spiritually drunk *(1 Samuel 1:13, Acts 2:15)* during my own praise and worship. Their pastor once told me that it was feminine. Another time, when I worshiped at a different church's tent meeting, a minister from the same apostolic church I had been attending since January 1995 was also visiting that night. And she said to me that I had demons and that my worship was an expression of demonic activity. But I was certain they were wrong. So, they did not stop me.

However, at the appointed time, GOD did send a Caucasian male apostle and a Caucasian female prophet to let me know that I was to learn to more appropriately worship GOD but to worship Him with my masculinity. Meaning for example, let's say a female who was groomed her entire childhood to be a lesbian. That female may have learned to express masculinity in her female body. So one day, GOD comes along and saves that now young adult female, yet just because that female accepted Christ, it does not mean no changes will need to soon be made in her life and her expression of worship. Up to receiving Christ, all she knew was being masculine. So, as GOD would teach her to worship, she would learn to do it as a female and with her femininity. GOD would help change her actions and ways, from her old lifestyle, and it will indeed affect her worship expression going forward. The same was true for me. GOD had to teach me to express my love for Him as a young man with my masculinity. It was not demonic worship. The female minister was wrong.

Churches must use wisdom and kindness when leading gender-confused people toward their destiny with GOD. It was feminine, yes, what people saw needed correcting. Yet they could not clearly discern what they saw or how to help it. So, rather than helping me, they both further added to my hurt and pain in my early twenties.

To assist with this training in masculinity, GOD sent certain GODly men into my life from Greater Bethel Temple and other local ministries. They all helped me by regularly being around them in person and on calls, to see what masculinity looked and sounded like. I watched their mannerisms and paid attention to them during praise and worship. My worship remained just as extreme and out of the ordinary, but it looked less and less feminine. And it became masculine.

"Are You A Lesbian?"

While still faithfully attending the same apostolic church in Louisville, I also worked the 3rd shift at Roadway Package Systems–now known as FedEx. Eventually, I worked at United Parcel Service (U.P.S.).

LaShonda Bowdre worked at U.P.S. and attended the same church I'd been going to. We formally met just inside the entrance of the church one day, and a strong friendship was the near immediate result.

We soon spent much time together at her parent's home, where she lived, or even at the house I rented from. We would even hold hands and pray on the floor at church in the early morning hours. We soon became inseparable. She would even buy me groceries when I had none or little, and we would often ride to work together in her red hatchback car, a Chevrolet. We quickly became best friends.

Then, one early weekday morning in 1997, I had a dream that I did not understand. Later that day, LaShonda's father, a prophet of GOD, was known back then for meeting with people at their homes, holding their hands, praying for them, and beginning to prophesy. Well, that night, he held LaShonda and my hands in their living room in a circle of prayer. He then soon prophesied

41

and told us we were to be married. My eyes popped open, as did hers, and I quickly decided that he was a false prophet. He then soon left the house, and we were left there confused and dazed.

Earlier that day, GOD had told me to attend a night service at a different church in the west end, where a visiting prophet was preaching. And while this prophet did not call me up to prophesy directly to me, he did, however, confirm The Word of The Lord that I was to marry LaShonda. Even in my dream from that morning, I later understood that GOD was telling me that she was my wife. That same night, as we prepared to go to work, a sudden protection of her came upon me. And from that day forward, the love we had already shared with each other multiplied. And we became more and more inseparable.

Many church people were against us and our expected marriage. We decided to tell the pastor of the same rather large apostolic church we both had been attending and met at, regarding our marital plans. So we arranged a meeting with him, and he said something startling to us. During that meeting, he said to us that when he first heard we were getting married, he said: "Not in my church." He told us this. He even pulled me out of the meeting and then proceeded to ask LaShonda a startling question. The pastor of the church where she was a member for years and where I had been attending since 1995 asked LaShonda if she was a lesbian. Quite apparently, he had decided that because, in his mind, I was a homosexual, he decided that she must be a practicing lesbian since she was seriously intending to marry me.

My mother even opposed our marriage. She told LaShonda not to marry me, very apparently because I was irresponsible and not keeping a job. I had been fired from U.P.S, I often got fired or quit a job when I wanted to or for unfounded reasons. It's probable that she didn't think I could be very reliable in a marriage.

Around that time, I was also a part of Greater Bethel Temple's prison ministry. Monthly, we went and ministered at North Point Prison in Kentucky. I had a speech impediment back then, a sort of stutter. It would surface when I ministered for some reason. But that dissipated eventually. During one ride to the prison to minister, two female ministers rode in the back of the vehicle with me. Both were suffering in their physical bodies. And I prayed for them there in the back seat. When we arrived at the service, they both testified over the pulpit that they were healed. I didn't know how much GOD would eventually use me. I just knew He was and would be even more.

Once, some friends and I visited a multi-ethnic church called Eagles Nest, which was very prophetic and lively with worship. The husband and wife pastored together. The wife–Prophetess Jan–prophesied to me one Sunday evening: "Now, son, I've called you to preach, prophesy, and raise the dead. Now teach." GOD had been talking to me a lot since 1995, but now He was revealing my gifts to others. While prophecy, preaching, and resurrection ministry were to come, at that time, I was to focus on teaching.

LaShonda and I agreed with GOD's order for our lives and prepared for marriage. While I was never allowed to be a member of that large apostolic church, I had remained faithful there for about three years, but by the spring of 1998, we had both joined Greater Bethel Temple, the church I was at when I recommitted my life to Christ in January of 1995.

That April, Apostle/Bishop Tudor Bismark of Harare, Zimbabwe, was there to minister four services in three days for the missionary department. During that first service, Apostle Bismark, before he even took a scripture, walked down to me on the crowded floor of the very large church. And he prophesied to me before everyone, as I sat next to my fiancée LaShonda. GOD said to me through the Apostle Bismark: "In you is the making of a prophet, a generating of anointing, that the devil is very envious of. You must walk very humbly before The Lord because pride will destroy what GOD is about to do in your life. You must walk very humbly before The Lord because what GOD is about to do in your life, only He could pull it off."

Apostle/Bishop Tudor Bismark said that and then touched my chest or stomach. When he did this, my prayer language *(Acts 2:4 and 1 Corinthians 12:28)* matured and advanced immediately.

The closer we come to GOD and His purpose for our lives, the more our gifts, including our prayer language, can grow from one stage to another. When Apostle Bismark laid hands on me, I grew spiritually. This would be the first of more encounters with this Apostle and Bishop.

Shortly thereafter, I founded and started H.E.L.P. - Helping Every Lame Person - Outreach Ministries. We held outreach

44

services at two Louisville-based Salvation Army shelters, a Boys and Girls Club, local nursing homes, a jail in Indiana, a jail in downtown Louisville, and a mental health hospital. I also had a gospel radio station ministry program and a weekly television program. My teaching ministry had started. By the summer of 1999, I held a conference at the Salvation Army, which drew a crowd for the services and classes we held that day and into that evening. It was evident that The Word, spoken through Apostle Bismark and Prophetess Jan, indicated that GOD had great plans for my life. Where would I go from there?

Like Rocks In My Belly

On Tuesday night, December 1, 1998, at her parent's home, with a total of about ten people in attendance, right there in the living room. We got married. On her wedding finger was a ring that was borrowed, and on my finger was a very thin and lightweight ring that I purchased at a pawn shop. Her father officiated the wedding. Her mother, who eventually came to love me deeply and dearly, at that time apparently believing that her daughter was making a huge mistake, seemed to be very depressed as she watched her husband marry her daughter and me. That Tuesday night, LaShonda and I became one, Husband and Wife.

Later that night, we hurried to our new apartment on the far other side of town. That was my first intercourse with a female. LaShonda had been celibate by then for seven years, so it was new for both of us. We had no furniture and slept on the floor for about a year, but we loved each other. She worked during the day for an insurance agency in downtown Louisville, and I worked sometimes at night, once at a Wal-Mart.

45

I had not been intimate with a male since I had returned to GOD in January of 1995. But one night, a good-looking young man came into Wal-Mart with his boyfriend into the electronics department where I was assigned to work. That young man made a pass at me while providing me with his telephone number. I soon called him and went to his place while his boyfriend was at work. While at his home, he pranced around in front of me, wearing tight shorts. But I felt convicted being there and left without giving in to his advances. But would that conviction last?

That year, our first year, LaShonda and I were getting to know each other a lot. LaShonda learned how inconsiderate I was. And she eventually learned not to cry when I showed my selfish and inconsiderate characteristics. She soon learned to speak up to me for herself. We grew in knowledge of one another, and while we did not have much, we did have each other.

I was also very busy with H.E.L.P. during the day while she was at work, and I often worked at night. So, life was full.

By December of that same year, GOD led LaShonda and me to move to Michigan, a place I had never even visited. So, we began traveling there weekly to see apartments and to apply for complexes. Finally, we were approved and moved there in December of 1999, one year into our marriage. We attended an apostolic church for some weeks in Ypsilanti, MI, but by early 2000, we joined Abyssinia Christ-Centered Ministries—A.C.C.M.

Nationally renowned Evangelist Dr. Iona E. Locke was the pastor of the church. Ten years prior, in 1990, I was filled with the Holy Ghost during her ministry in Lexington. I knew I was home while praying, lying on the floor during their Wednesday night prayer service. When Dr. Locke invited me to close out the prayer in the pulpit. I knew I was home and not an outcast there. I was known to pray loudly. She wanted my sort of prayer prayed over the pulpit in everyone's hearing.

Soon, Dr. Locke told me one day in her office that GOD was talking to her about me. I understood this to mean that GOD was advising her that He had a purpose for me at ACCM.

By then I had become busy preaching for ACCM during their outreach ministries on Saturdays. And during that summer of 2000, Dr. Locke called on me to preach for the Sunday morning main service on youth day. I was ecstatic for the opportunity. Some of my family from Lexington even drove up to attend in support of me. Afterward, Dr. Locke continued to call on me to minister. I preached other services, even when she was away ministering.

Still, during that summer of 2000, I was very active with the outreach ministry. One Saturday, we had a day of more extensive and planned outreach next to a shelter where we often ministered. And the outreach ministry leadership called on me to minister often that day. Before the services began, Dr. Locke warned me and the other ministers to wear visors to protect us from the sun. She also told us to eat during the day to avoid exhaustion. However, that whole day, I barely ate, if at all, and I never wore a sports cap. By that evening outside in the service, I was bending over a heavy-set lady, rebuking her demons, and praying. And she suddenly became dizzy looking and dazed, with her eyes focused on me. Her eyes seemed to hypnotize me. It was like a demon was working magic on me through her – like a spell was being cast on and into me. Very suddenly, I became heavy, as if I had stones in my belly. And I was immediately weak and had to be assisted to someone's van to rest. I could minister no more that day.

That whole night at home, I felt very heavy, like huge rocks were inside of my belly. The very next day, Sunday morning, while in Dr. Locke's office suite with other ministers, she asked me if I was okay before service began. I lied, saying yes. Then, during praise and worship service, as I stood worshiping GOD, I began to burp, and I kept on burping. The more I burped, the more I felt relief. The lighter I felt. By the end of that Sunday service, I was delivered from the demons that had gained access to my body through disobedience and rebellion to Dr. Locke's directives.

As quickly as GOD had elevated me at Abyssinia, my pride demoted me. I was filled with pride, and I could not handle the quick promotion that was taking place. So, as soon as Dr. Locke began giving me ministry exposure and opportunity, it was also that soon that she sat me down, which is when I manifested even more immaturity.

Around then, I grew close to a young man at ACCM who was gay. We became intimate as I began to get close to him. He and I would spend long periods of time flirting with one another over the telephone, specifically when I was working the first shift in an office and had lots of time to spare on the phone. We were hardly ever physically intimate, but our emotional bond was extreme and strong. Emotional bonding can be just as damaging

48

as physical bonding. LaShonda had her ideas that he and I were being sexual, but she could never prove it. I was very manipulative and a great liar.

In my immaturity and great carnality from continued homosexual bonding, thus being opened to portals of demonic gifts given by familiar spirits due to disobedience and unholy alliance, I once gave what I believed GOD was saying, a Word of Knowledge *(1 Corinthians 12:8)*, to a relative of Dr. Locke. This relative and their mother did not receive nor appreciate it. So they took it to Pastor Locke, and she chastised me for it. This added to a wall that separated me from more ministry opportunities at ACCM. The promotion was over there, but not permanently.

Countless men and women are called, gifted, and ordained by GOD to prophesy and do many things for His glory, but there is an order *(1 Corinthians 14:40)*. We must be humble enough to follow a chain of command. I was reckless with my gift. And while GOD had called me, when I chose to submit to sin, the devil's gifts likely unknowingly opened up to me. Whatever the source of the word to Dr. Locke's relative, whether GOD or the devil, the wisest thing I could have done would have been to leave sin alone, to stop bonding with a homosexual.

Sin blinds us to the truth, and when we think we helped people and gave them a Word from The Lord, we may very well be hurting them. That word could be from the devil.

I did eventually seem to reach a point when things were going well in marriage and ministry at times, so it seemed. But I still kept getting in the way of my success. Still, though, I was pressing on despite my errors. Whether it was my marriage, ministry, or employment issues, I was in it for better or worse.

So, around the fall of 2001, I had stopped bonding with that homosexual. I and was not entertaining other gay men either. And while living in a tiny condominium that we rented from a church member by then, we began having Bible study one night a week. Due to nonpayment, we had been evicted from our first Michigan apartment complex. So, a church brother helped us out with a property he owned. Soon, I informed Dr. Locke that GOD was leading me to start a church, and she permitted me to go forth. It began in the condo's small living room with friends I invited and family they invited with them. I was now learning what it meant to pastor my second ministry: Master Builders Ministries, Int'l.

CHAPTER 4
SPIRITUAL BATTLES AND PERSONAL GROWTH

He Apologized To Me

While in that condo, LaShonda returned home from work one day to see an Altoid breath mint on the bedroom floor. And she concluded that I had been intimate with someone in our condo, which was actually false. Nothing ever happened there with me and a guy. Consequently, she tried to hold me hostage in that small unit as I tried to convince her that I was not guilty. So, I had to leave in my boxers in order to escape. That was the first time we became physical with one another in anger. If I had not left, the outcome would have been much worse. But that would not be the last physical interaction between her and me.

Upon my arrival in Michigan, I also started an online ministry called 'His Mouthpiece Ministries.' I had a large and growing audience that received my emails daily and then weekly, which contained a prophetic Word from The Lord. That was where The Lord first began to teach me how to communicate effectively through writing. So, in addition to pastoring Master Builders Ministries, Int'l, which later was changed to Greater Works

International Ministries, I also preached online through writing. But while ministering, I would eventually once again entertain the lustful appetite that was ever-growing inside of me.

Whether we engage and mingle in sin periodically or often, it was after that initial sexual encounter and constant homosexual bonding with the guy from Dr. Locke's church that the desire began to multiply within me once again for the same sex. As I stated before, Satan is patient, and he will keep working to overthrow us and the will of GOD in our lives, no matter how long it takes him.

By 2002, I was still pastoring. We were holding services in a building near downtown Detroit on Thursdays. Some people from the shelter in the area and also young children attended with their adult relatives.

That same year, in the midst of the back and forth struggling with homosexuality, I don't remember why I approached Dr. Locke to confess to her. I can't recall who I was with, whether on the phone, on video, or in person at a park I would frequent sometimes. However, I know that I told her. I admitted to her that I had engaged in homosexual activity. I set up a meeting with her. And as soon as I met her for that appointment, she walked over to me and rebuked "perversion" from me. Almost immediately, I began to vomit up a mixture of blood—indicating what I believe to be a generational curse—along with other liquids. It lay there on the floor of her pearl-colored carpet. After that, I went downstairs to the sanctuary altar and continued to repent before The Lord. I left there thankful and free indeed. But it would not last long.

Maybe a year later, after we had moved to Madison Heights, Michigan, I had familiarized myself with sex phone lines, where you could meet people over the phone for sexual involvements. And I soon learned about another mostly ethnic popular website where you could meet people of even other nationalities and locations and then exchange phone numbers. When LaShonda was asleep in the back bedroom, I would be in the living room, often having phone sex with total strangers. The devil sought to fill my time with constant homosexual interactions, and I allowed him to fill it.

During those times of much same-sex contact, I met an Apostle online who was, at the time, struggling like I was with his own sexual appetites. We quickly became intimate on the phone together. He lived in New Jersey at that time. Soon after our interactions, he repented and got right with GOD. Before I continue, let me say this: Just because you struggle, it doesn't mean GOD can't use you. So, while on a call with him one night, this Apostle began to rebuke the devil from me. And after the call ended that whole night, I was throwing up, vomiting, and being purged as GOD was ridding me of demons. That would not be the last time that demons would have to leave me.

Sin can have access to many areas of our lives. Sin can defeat us and our progress in ways we never thought possible. While I was unknowingly being intimate with demons, through masturbating often on the phone and video sex, I was still intimate with LaShonda. I had decided to be down low, keeping my homosexual appetite on the low and under the surface, all the while preaching and prophesying. I never much considered how being sexual with her could spread what I let inside of me, inside of her, too. To be sexual is to be spiritual as well. Sex is far more than a physical act. Sex has the power and complete capability to pass a demon spirit from one person to the next.

In approximately 2003, we had our first miscarriage. She miscarried physically and emotionally, but I was united with the baby, too, so it was our miscarriage. It was an emotional miscarrying for me. The baby we named Madison was born at 14 weeks. It was a devastating loss. Sometime later, we had another miscarriage, which was a blood clot flushed down the toilet. She had been pregnant for a very short period of time. Later, she had to have a dilation and curettage procedure (DNC) to get the fetus' remains out of her womb.

Another powerful thing that occurred around this time of about 2004 was when GOD gave me a vision while living in Madison Heights, Michigan. The vision was about Louisville, Kentucky. The dream was directed to church leaders in Louisville. It gave me insight to share with them and into handling what GOD showed me was happening in the city. I was led to call several Louisville pastors, including the pastor of the rather large apostolic church that I had attended from 1995 to 1998.

On that call to him, I shared what GOD showed me. To my amazement, he received wholeheartedly what I had to say, telling me that it confirmed what GOD showed him. Then, I had an opportunity to tell him how hurt he and his church made me feel years prior. This man - this changed man - without me even asking, he apologized to me on behalf of the whole church. This pastor and now bishop humbled himself. His apology meant to me that my life had come full circle. That call healed a part of me. GOD healed me, which had been needed years prior. To GOD be the glory!

Growing But In The Wrong Direction

As much as I would serve GOD but continually backslide, GOD was still good to me. He continued to provide. While still holding church services near downtown Detroit, by the spring of 2005, I was given an extreme opportunity, along with a list of phone numbers and a script, to call senior citizens in metropolitan Detroit to persuade them to partake in home health care through agencies that I eventually contracted with.

I was very good at this work, and I was paid $1,000 for my first eight or nine hours of calls made. I had hit the jackpot, so I thought. I began making a lot of money and soon hired other telemarketers. Very soon, my wife and I were able to relocate from our two-bedroom Madison Heights apartment to a much larger two-level plus basement townhome in Warren, MI.

In 2005, my daughter, Jade, was also conceived. GOD was blessing us. Things were finally happening for us.

By this time, I was likely not practicing homosexuality much or at all. And GOD, in his kind mercy, blessed and still used me, even in my wrong doing. He does this with us. He blesses and still uses us, even when we're wrong.

Matthew 5:45b (KJV)

"...for He (The Lord) maketh His sun to rise on the evil and on the good, and sendeth rain on the just and on the unjust."

Romans 11:29 (KJV)

"For the gifts and calling of GOD are without repentance."

We must realize that GOD has chosen to pour blessings on those who are unjust, too. And allows them to use their GOD-given gifts and calling, even when they have not yet repented. I am certain that He does not want us to remain in sin. But it is written in The Bible, so it is a law and fact.

I was often wicked in my ways, and I very often chose sin, but He blessed me and used my ministry anyway. But that would not last forever.

That same year, I joined under the leadership of Apostle and Bishop Tudor Bismark and Jabula International Network (J.I.N). He is the same apostle who publicly identified my approaching prophetic office back in 1998. For the first time, I was licensed and ordained that same year of 2005. I had never been installed or ordained under Bishop Locke. She respected and would refer to me as a pastor and prophet, but I did not meet her qualifications to be ordained due to a lack of adequate membership in my church, according to her standards. So, while I did have ups and downs, while under her leadership, I left her network Christ Centered Ministries Assemblies–CCMA–on good terms, and I joined JIN, along with the church I pastored, Greater Works International Ministries.

That same year, I was invited to preach out of state for the first time. I was flown to Baltimore, Maryland. I was given a whopping $1,400 offering, and I felt like I was in the best place, ministry-wise and financially, I had ever been in. Meanwhile, I continued to develop and network for the telemarketing business I had started, Trumbo Consulting Agency–TCA–connecting senior citizens with visiting doctors and home healthcare agencies. While doing all of this, I still repeatedly and regularly entertained and engaged in homosexuality, mostly through a very popular gay website at that time.

Jade was born on Saturday, April 11, 2006, at 26 weeks and three days, afterward spending two months in the hospital, mostly in the neonatal intensive care unit–NICU.

Some weeks later, I had been sexual with a young man some miles from Warren, MI, and I ended up with a hickey on my neck, which LaShonda found out about the same day. It devastated her, but I vowed it would not happen again, and I lied, saying that there was only kissing. All of that was very obviously a lie– but I was exceptional at falsifying things. So she chose to forgive me, and we moved forward after leaders within JIN held a ceremony with us, where our rings were cleaned as an act of a new start. As for TCA, I continued pursuing new business contracts, and it continued to grow financially and with new employees.

Greater Works International Ministries soon held services in a storefront church in Detroit, but we never grew to more than maybe fifteen parishioners. I was much too absorbed with money and men to focus much on GWIM. At one point, LaShonda and I had over $100K in the bank, though we were not very wise with our finances.

I also had a terrible attitude and I was cocky and hateful with various offices that TCA worked with. So, while they loved the money I made them, they despised my arrogant attitude. So TCA was exploding with cash, but perversion and pride were exploding, too, inside of me.

A newly introduced non gay huge social media platform and other social media still gave me many opportunities to engage with others who had a homosexual nature and appetite like mine, especially other Christians who were attracted to the same sex.

Homosexuality Can Never Love

Around 2009, I closed the doors of Greater Works International Ministries. It was hard for me to do marriage, men, TCA, and pastoring.

In 2010, I took our ministry back under the leadership of Bishop Iona Locke and CCMA, and she welcomed me back with open arms and soon ordained me as well. I was not actively pastoring at that time, but I expected I would, so she did ordain me.

In early 2010, we began to visit Virginia, near Washington DC, as LaShonda and I knew that GOD was calling us to relocate there. However, during one visit to view properties, a hotel manager and I were intimate in one of the hotel rooms. Perversion had become regular for me no matter where I was. Still, GOD continued to bless me, so it seemed. We moved to Stafford, Virginia in June 2010.

By then, I often made ten thousand or more dollars a week through TCA. Because the business was mainly telemarketing, I did not have to live in Michigan. I could live anywhere and run my business. And by then, I had about thirty employees, mostly telemarketers, who lived in different states. More money than I'd ever had was constantly coming to me.

With some money, I took out advertisements to help start a new ministry, using the most popular Washington DC area's gospel radio station, Radio One's 104.1 FM. I shortly started a Thursday night service from those ads. Many people replied to those advertisements, which attracted people who wanted the prophetic, and soon, the small hotel meeting room was packed to capacity. Still, I was many things, but not a holy man. I was a financially prosperous man but not a holy man. A pastor but not a holy man. A husband and father but not a holy man.

With my own intuition and not GOD's, I soon moved our ministry from that Marriott Hotel in Woodbridge, Virginia, to Alexandria, a city just outside of Washington DC, but still in Virginia. There in another hotel, we had Sunday services instead of Thursdays. No matter how hard I worked and monetarily gave to this new ministry, Open Heaven Ministries International (OHMI), I would allow GOD to lead me in some areas but not others. My lack of consistent submission to GOD caused me, OHMI, and my family to suffer and eventually be very limited and very constricted.

What we do does, in fact, affect others and every area of our own life. I chose to be a daily hypocrite who still dated and was intimate with men every step of the way. Because of such hypocrisy, nothing seemed to improve my attempts and strategies to move the church forward. All of the progress for OHMI seemed to halt all at once. We were in a new space but seemed eventually to be standing still. This standstill and even regression would also soon occur for TCA.

Sin is normally anxious and in a hurry. It wants to destroy you as quickly as possible. With that said, sometime before leaving Michigan, I had hired an "apostle" who worked for me, but he was also my boyfriend. One time, I took a trip to Florida, where he lived, only to fulfill the lust of my flesh, even preaching for his ministry while there. Looking back, I realize I wanted him to work for me so I would have additional excuses for all of the times we had to talk and spend together.

Later, while residing in Virginia, I repeated the same, employing a man I met online. We very quickly became intimate with one another. He was originally from North Carolina and was slightly older than me. He was a student at a university in Bowie, Maryland, where he was studying to be an accountant. He was highly intelligent. I felt inseparable from him early on. He was the first person since Tyrone in 1994; he was the first person that I had 'complete sex' with now there in 2011. That was also around the time that LaShonda and I soon began seeing a marriage counselor because we were constantly at odds with one another. I chose to be an entrepreneur, pastor, prophet, husband, and father, all the while being a homosexual and committing adultery.

He and I would take business trips together. They were usually business trips, too, but it was ultimately about getting away to be homosexually active under the guise of business. Eventually, he and I learned to loathe each other because I could be very mean and hateful, even towards him.

The thing that I now understand is that I was taking on the characteristics of multiple people. You see, when we sexually sin, other demons can easily enter us through those sins. And it's easily possible to take on the characteristics of people we have sex with. The more that I had some form of sex with this intelligent aspiring account, and soon with so many other gay and bisexual men throughout Virginia, Maryland, and Washington, DC, other demons were entering me too. I was not just sexual with these people, but I was sexual with the demons that infested them.

He was my operations manager, or so we called his title. I paid him vast sums of money, which was very wasteful of me. The devil wanted me to be promiscuous and broke, and he was achieving his goal. Additionally, our intimate life eventually dwindled, as I suspected he was cheating on me. We very regularly had verbal fights. I suspect it was also because more mean spirits were beginning to live inside of me. He and I lasted from about 2011 till about 2013.

When lust is at the center, it will never last. We were bound to end. Lust alone cannot last. If lust is at the core and center, it cannot last. And homosexuality is never born out of love, only lust. Homosexuality cannot love, it can only lust.

After he and I broke up, I went on many trips alone for play and for work-related meetings. I traveled to Florida, Georgia, Texas, and Illinois, spending loads of money and being sexual while en route and once I arrived at my destination. I often would leave one household having been sexual with a man, and then via various dating apps, I'd find more sex 30 minutes to an hour later. Lust can never get enough.

Meanwhile, LaShonda and I would argue very regularly at home. We were becoming more and more distant as I was not there for her emotionally.

I repeatedly, because of various sexual acts, became maneuvered by demons. I would be hateful, mean, and nasty to my wife. I was increasingly out of control. I had sexual interactions with countless men, countless, all while being married to LaShonda. And my business was also coming towards a financial collapse in late 2013. I even ended up with crabs, body lice, again. Destruction was happening.

Preaching With An STD

Homosexuality is authored and controlled by a demon spirit. It is introduced to mankind through opportunities, which normally begin with thoughts and ideas. And the devil desires to rule man even through their sexuality.

I was never content long-term or even often short-term with any one male. If I wasn't masturbating to porn or having sex with others on the phone or video, I was still ignoring LaShonda's intimate needs. And if I wasn't having sex through the phone, I was making time to meet other men in person for sexual purposes.

"Robert" was a prophet and friend whom I had known for some years, and he introduced me to popular phone applications used to seek out homosexuals. These apps offer quick meet-ups to men in the area where you are currently or even plan to visit.

These apps were additional doorways to creating and seemingly fulfilling more and more lusts in my flesh. I was satisfied, at least temporarily, or so I thought. I would tell LaShonda that I was out tending to business or for outreach ministries, but I was often somewhere meeting my sexual desires. Over time, more and more and more demons entered my body, attaching to my soul.

These apps were my habit and constant go-to. So while I ran TCA, pastored OHMI, fathered Jade, and was a very partial husband to LaShonda, I regularly went from one location to the next being intimate with men. Often, I had more than one or two partners at separate times in one day, sometimes three of us together. I was given over to same-sex sin. I was a lustful sex addict. Washington, DC, Maryland, and Virginia are also havens for homosexuals, and I made the best of it. And I continued to feed the demons I had invited into me all while letting new ones in.

Toward the end of 2013, and no longer with my business partner and boyfriend, TCA struggled, and so did OHMI, as did my marriage. The only thing winning and succeeding during those times was homosexuality. I could not competently manage and multi-task all of those responsibilities plus sin. I was so perverted and trapped in sin that whether I was away ministering or on anniversary trips, I would find the ways and means to feed my hunger, to be same-sexually active. I gave in to these lusts over and over and over again. It was nonstop.

LaShonda eventually became a coverup, as did the ministry, to a degree, but I did not see that then.

With no official boyfriend, I just wanted homosexuality. A relationship didn't matter ultimately, but sex did. The needs of that indwelling spirit in me were even more important to me than money. So much so that throughout 2013, I had paid less and less attention to TCA and more to my lusts.

Within TCA and unbeknownst to me, I had people working for me, and starting the same kind of marketing business I had of their own, often with patients and clients that they stole from me. This activity affected me significantly financially. It was as if one day, I just woke up and realized that the rug of economic stability and strength had been pulled from underneath me.

By December 2013, I could barely afford what was so easy to pay just twelve months previously. I could no longer afford the high-end cars we were driving, the mortgage, the daycare, more of the previously taken trips to Puerto Rico, California, Las Vegas, Hawaii, multiple Florida trips, or the housekeeping service. The constant big spending had come to a halt.

Giving in to sin, lust, and perversion had depleted my money. And oddly, I did not care like I should have because if I had, I would have focused on TCA much more. But when I let demons in, the chief of those spirits controlled my life. While greed was a demon, I had; the chief demons were perversion and homosexuality. So money did matter, but sex mattered more. Sex mattered a whole lot more.

The level of perversion got so extreme that I even invited men to my home and even to my church office to be sexual with, right there on the office floor or in other rooms. I was so dominated by homosexual acts that one early Sunday morning, I went to the home of a bodily attractive man. And I could plainly see that he had a STD on his body part. But sin makes people stupid. I was so stupid back then. So, we were intimate anyway. Soon after that, on another Sunday morning, likely the next, I was at a clinic getting a shot for chlamydia. Then, I went to church and preached the same afternoon. I did make sure not to be intimate with LaShonda during that span of time.

Sin costs, it costs, it costs. But it costs much more than money and a STD.

Sin also deceives. I honestly felt that I could make it work because I had the anointing, a wife, a daughter, TCA, OHMI, and the gift and office of prophecy. I believed that GOD would remain patient with me, as I felt he was with others who I believed were in sin like myself. I believed He would give me more time to repent of my sins. I didn't realize then that He would eventually give me "time," and plenty of it, in the approaching years.

New Opportunities But The Same Lifestyle

Economically, in distress and financial turmoil, by the beginning of 2014, I decided that I needed to repent to be blessed again. I figured that my money, church, and marriage were all struggling and even cursed. So that whole year, the church OHMI and I went on a fast together. We would fast on the last and first day of every month. And it worked! GOD began to bless my finances once again!

65

In retrospect, I completely believe it was GOD giving me another chance due to fasting and focusing on Him. Often in the scriptures, we read that when people turn towards GOD, He listens, answers, and favors them once again *(2 Chronicles 7:13-14)*. It worked! But it would not keep working.

That entire year of 2014, I stayed away from any sexual acts with men. But as soon as GOD responded to me with blessings and economic growth by very early 2015, I backslid again.

There was a pastor of a large Baptist congregation in Maryland who wanted me to provide him with sexual favors in his car once a week. I consented. To return the "favor," he regularly advised me on how to jump-start OHMI. He became like a pastoral mentor to me. I even told LaShonda about him, but not about what I was doing in the car.

Having been unable to eventually afford the hotels we rented and the commercial space we later rented, by 2015, we had services in our townhome and other members' homes. It was working, so it seemed. And that Baptist pastor seemed to be doing well with his church, though his marriage was on the brink of divorce. So, I felt I could succeed and be a pastor, too. So, I dated him and others in 2015, all simultaneously. Dating for me meant spending time, and eventually or often, sexual time with each of them.

So, despite the pause in 2014 from homosexuality, during the year 2015, I was back in "love" with sin and perversion and men. And during the summer of 2015, I shut the doors of OHMI. Most of the approximately thirty members I had were just too inconsistent in some way or another. So I decided I could not afford to pastor anymore. I also had already stopped seeing the Baptist pastor. Consequently, I had more time to get involved with more sin and lust. I had my consistent men for phone sex and on-cam video masturbation.

Around then, TCA was struggling more than it ever had. It had previously been so very easy to make large amounts of money, and now I could barely make ends meet.

Aside from closing OHMI and an imploding TCA, I had weekly teleconferences, which I had already started conducting years before. In the fall of 2015, I was made aware of Periscope. It was owned by Twitter (now X), and it was the first colossal platform to offer live-stream videos, allowing me to minister to a live audience. Even in my sins, ministry was necessary. When I ministered, it was also an opportunity for GOD to tell me to repent. So, I needed to minister. It helped to save me, even if not until later on.

I would preach on Periscope to an international audience four mornings a week for 3-4 hours straight, plus a teleconference one night a week. The audience grew larger, with some 200 people or more often watching me simultaneously. TCA was still struggling, so I welcomed and sometimes solicited offerings I would receive from the live viewers.

The Lord would use me in a mighty way. As a result of this online Periscope ministry, in late 2015, an intermediate pastor of the apostolic church I grew up in, in Lexington, Kentucky, invited me to preach there. GOD used me even there. But gifts and callings are without repentance *(Romans 11:29)*. I had learned

67

to look far past my daily sins to preach, prophesy, and inspire others with The Word of The Lord. All the while still allowing demons to enter my life, body, soul, and mind.

CHAPTER 5
FALLING INTO DARKNESS

Not Wanting To Let The Demons Go

By late 2015 and 2016, I wasn't nearly as active homosexually as I had been in 2010-2013. But I had still not repented. So, The Lord began to come at me from another direction, and I knew nothing about it.

By the summer of 2016, a nurse practitioner who previously benefited me financially a lot began to be seemingly bipolar and to turn against me. Weeks later, and unknown to me, a Pakistanian, the then owner of a rather large Michigan-based Home Healthcare agency, began to conceal conversations with me. These conversations were regarding kickbacks I was being paid per patient for clients I provided for his agency's home healthcare services. I had actually discontinued working with his agency as directed by The Holy Spirit years before. However, being very much in need financially, I contacted him to reconnect and work together again around 2014 because he had once been very loyal financially.

So, by the fall of 2016, our home was in the process of very likely foreclosure, and I was greatly concerned about that, as expected. And I wasn't paying much attention to business calls. And this agency owner unusually called me one day, naming clients I provided to his agency. He talked about how much he would pay me for those clients accepting his agency's home healthcare services. These were called kickbacks and are illegal in that line of work. The FBI had directed him to contact me and others as well. He was in much more trouble for about 20 million in healthcare fraud. So, he was looking at a very lengthy prison sentence. So, he became a "snitch" to get a reduced sentence by revealing my fraud-related business dealings with him and his home health agency. But this plot would not be known to me until over a year later. Though, by early 2017, I knew that his company was under investigation by the government, but I had decided that it had nothing to do with me.

Around the spring of 2017, LaShonda and I short-sold our home to avoid foreclosure, and we moved into a rented townhouse. But even with all of this struggle, I continued to remain in sinful disobedience, still hooking up with men for the act of sexual satisfaction, getting drunk, and repeatedly masturbating via video on an app with total strangers. I was so bound by these acts that I was once so very close to getting caught by LaShonda.

In northern Virginia, I would often attend a spa, a nude spa, where individuals were only allowed to be naked there. Supposedly, it was family-friendly and even legal. But that place was a cesspool for sexual misbehavior, whether it happened there or after men met there.

By November 2017, I became more transparent on my Facebook Live videos (Facebook Lives had replaced Periscope live streams). The Lord used me to tell my story about facing my own Goliath–sexual immorality. I was sharing, but only to a degree, as I did not really want to let the demons go. I would be deceptive, pretending that the struggle was the past, and not still the present. I spoke out like that because by then, I actually had much left those same-sex actions alone. I still had a fondness for them, but I was not nearly as focused on it as I had been in times past. I had even stopped in-person sexual acts with men.

During that fall, I started a ministry/school of prophets, The Ecclesia, which grew in number but often drew people with the wrong motives or expectations.

The Ecclesia and the Facebook Lives were lifelines, repeatedly giving me an opportunity to minister to myself and others what all GOD expected of me. But they didn't work eventually.

Countdown To Prison

The date was Thursday, December 21, 2017. I was no longer pastoring, and TCA was still failing economically, and I was still a whoremonger, even if not with men in person. LaShonda and I, through a newly obtained credit card, could afford to take our daughter Jade to Disney World. We had taken her there multiple times and on many other vacations since she was a baby.

That Thursday morning, I received a call from an unknown number out of state. The caller left a message that it was the FBI. When I returned his call, he talked about how the home health agency, owned by the Pakistani, was in legal trouble and that they knew I was connected with him. My heart sank as I determined quickly that life, as I knew it, had ended.

Having returned home, I talked to the FBI again. Shortly thereafter, a U.S. Marshall from Richmond, Virginia, served me with official documents at home worded with the possible intent to indict me. As usual, I began to repent once again before The Lord. However, none of this was actual repentance.

Repentance is a decision of the heart that affects our actions. Real repentance makes changes. It begins and continues to do right. All I did was beg GOD to help me without changing my heart.

After obtaining court-appointed legal counsel by April 2018, I decided that I would not be indicted. However, I did not realize that I had upset the government when I refused to cooperate with the FBI through my legal counsel and inform them of other people who had defrauded healthcare with me. So I believed that I wouldn't be indicted, especially since I didn't hear back from them. I felt I was okay. And, right after that decision, I went right back to a life of sin. I didn't see men sexually in person, but I was acting out perversion nonetheless.

By mid-June of 2018, having relocated to Lexington, Kentucky, unable to afford rent at the Virginia townhouse and temporarily staying with my parents, LaShonda and Jade, I got another call. My court-appointed public defender called me. And he informed me that I was due in Detroit the following week to be arraigned, indicted, charged with medicare fraud charges. Once again, I "repented." And days before the trip to Michigan, GOD told me in a bathroom at my parents home: "I will deliver you." These words gave me something to hold on to, not knowing exactly what "deliver" actually meant.

For months after that, the federal prosecutor's office provided my attorney with "discovery." Discovery was the evidence against me, and there was plenty of it. I was so filled with anxiety, going to my mailbox and sometimes receiving video, audio, text, and email evidence, the discovery of many conversations I'd had with the agency owner and others about home health care kickbacks.

By the winter of 2018, they added a wire fraud charge, very apparently because I refused to cooperate with the federal government, plead guilty, and become a snitch for them. This particular charge carried up to 20 years on its own. The other charges of Medicare fraud and conspiracy to commit Medicare fraud typically carried a sentence of five years. So I had to live day in and out, with the understanding that there was a strong possibility that I would receive a very lengthy sentence. But I chose to believe that just as GOD would deliver me from the lesser charges, He would also deliver me from the much more significant charge.

By then, we lived in a rented apartment and attended my cousin's husband's church. There, I was received and respected as a prophet. However, I wasn't traveling to places to preach anymore as in times past.

By the spring or summer of 2019, my father-in-law, Pastor Leonard, was ill after suffering from more than one stroke, and my brother-in-law, Deion, was near death. He had been on dialysis for years. In June, my brother Deion passed, and I was on trial the last week of July 2019. Such a troublesome and anxiety-consuming summer it was for LaShonda and for me.

On Tuesday, July 30, 2019, I was found innocent of wire fraud but guilty of Medicare fraud and conspiracy to commit Medicare fraud. The judge was fair and thorough. The evidence against me was overwhelming for Medicare fraud. I had never committed any sort of wire fraud, so that finding of innocence was accurate. Consequently, that drive home was my life's worst and longest ride, and I contemplated suicide as the ride continued.

On the way home to Kentucky from Michigan, I texted family and friends, telling them what had happened. None of them knew I had been on trial, let alone that I was found guilty. I spent the next several days being comforted by family, as they were very concerned due to my statements of contemplated suicide.

To treat that anguish, I did what I usually did. I turned back to sin and homosexuality. I spent about an entire month with pornography and personal pleasure. However, I chose not to interact with any male in person. After about 30 days, I stopped pleasuring myself, expecting GOD to get me out of this mess if I chose to sin sexually no more.

We are often quick to try and prove to GOD that we will do His will. When the truth is, there is nothing GOD does not know. So, while I may have convinced myself that I was suddenly righteous, He knew that until I truly repented, none of this was actual, and it would not endure long term.

As the sentencing date speedily approached, the week before Christmas 2019, I heard The Lord say the date would change. So, after we traveled to Michigan and sat there in the courtroom, the judge suddenly and very unusually rescheduled the date. Once the date changed to my prophetic knowing, GOD said: "I'm in charge. I'm running this." Ultimately, several dates had changed to my prophetic hearing in order to cause me to know that I, and this test, was in the hands of GOD, not man's, the judge, or a jury. So, I grew more confident that I was not to worry because GOD was entirely in control. No matter if I had been found guilty and was a convicted felon, He was still in charge.

Since GOD could tell me things that came to pass, I knew I could trust Him with everything else He'd told me in life. Still, I had not repented and I held onto sin in my heart.

GOD is so kind, and His love for us fails not. His love for me all those years never went anywhere. He will never turn His back on us. I knew then and now know that whether we are in sin or not, His love continues. During that time in my life, He continued to comfort, console, and add to me peace of mind. Thank GOD for His love. Thank GOD for His unfailing continued love.

On Thursday, February 6, 2020, right before COVID-19 largely hit the U.S., I was sentenced in open court to 60 months (5 years) for my felonious crimes. The judge overseeing my case had been the Honorable 36th District Court Chief Judge Denise Page-Hood, a woman of color whose husband is a prominent pastor. She is very fair, consistent, and competent, having graduated from Yale the same year I was born.

Chief Judge Hood received letters seeking a lenient sentence on my behalf, even from my pastor, the now late Bishop Iona E. Locke, D.D. Th.D. But the fair judge gave me five years anyway. I expect leniency is more for those who don't force a trial. Of course, I chose a trial, though I knew I was guilty. And while that drive back to Kentucky from Michigan was hard, at least my mother was with LaShonda and me for that ride. So, I just chose to trust and believe in GOD. I stayed away from homosexual acts and sought after GOD as my incarceration date approached, and COVID seemed to rule the world.

Information got out somehow of my indictment, conviction, and sentencing, though it seemed only to be known to people in my local area of Lexington, Kentucky. I tried not to think of my family and friends knowing my fate, and people purposely didn't discuss it with me. Meanwhile, I spent my days preaching online, having been laid off from work due to COVID-19. I was collecting unemployment and just waiting. I waited to go away, still having hope that I would never actually go away to prison.

I Turned My Back On LaShonda And Jade

On Monday, September 14, 2020, my wife, LaShonda, and mother, Betty, dropped me off to begin a five-year journey away from freedom.

Whether a person goes away for 5 months or 15 years, it always feels like forever. Denied freedom is a tremendous punishment.

While I did believe in GOD - well to me, I did - I chose, rather speedily, to engage in lust and perversion once again.

Due to COVID, I was quarantined in a cell for three weeks with a white guy, and within days, having not sexually known a man in person since 2017, I was very slightly intimate with him. Old habits die hard. It only happened once or twice during those three weeks. Despite being so incompatible, it still happened. When you have no other choices, you may settle for anything.

Sin doesn't take much.

Galatians 5:9 (KJV)

"A little leaven leaveneth the whole lump."

Song of Solomon 2:15 (KJV)

"Take us the foxes, the little foxes, that spoil the vines: for our vines have tender grapes."

A little leaven leavens the entire lump, and a little fox destroys the vine. Even a little sin will cause much damage.

The guy I was in quarantine with was admittedly suicidal and taking Buspirone, a drug to treat anxiety generally and possibly depression. After being minimally intimate with him, little did I know that I would be the same (suicidal) and on the same drug about one year later. You can easily become what/who you are sexual with. The interactions between him and I were short, incomplete, and most would say not even sexual at all. But when you open up to a spirit, whether you complete sex or not, you are possibly able to be overthrown by the demon you engage. Because more than a person, it's a spirit and more than you are with that individual, you are engaging their demon spirit(s).

After three weeks alone with him, I was led out of the prison cell in quarantine. Across the street from the Ashland, KY Satellite Camp was an actual Federal Corrections Prison, where I had to quarantine first. So, I began my punishment of incarceration at the prison camp in Ashland, a minimum-security facility about two hours east of Lexington.

I chose to begin this journey disconnected from spiritual responsibility both to others and to myself. It was as if I left my ministry and all spirituality on September 14, 2020. I think I felt I was even on a vacation from GOD. Sure, I would pray. I would cry out to GOD to get me through, but there was no sincere thirst for Him. None of it was from within. I was not connected to GOD by then. I had learned to play GOD and religion very well. I wanted His assistance and His help to make me feel better, but I didn't want Him. And He knew this.

While I was in quarantine those weeks in the Federal Corrections Prison, LaShonda sent me love letters, which I didn't retrieve until after I went to the camp. But all of that was about to change, all of it.

I had left my phone with her so she could access my CashApp and PayPal for whomever sent money, and to reach out to my contacts. There were no porn or X-rated sites that I had visited anytime recently. Yet, within weeks of my departure, she began to search my phone and came upon two conversations with men. These conversations were not very incriminating, but they still proved that I was, at the very least, still interested in a secret homosexual life. This completely broke LaShonda, causing her to know that I had been a liar, deceptive, and constantly manipulating her. And on our 22nd marriage anniversary, Tuesday, December 1, 2020, on a phone call, she wept and cried and wailed in such deep pain, telling me what she found on my mobile device. Of course, I apologized and pretended to care a lot when I was only sorry I was caught again. But by January 2021, she told me she was looking into divorce. So, I just chose to believe GOD and that she loved me too much to ever divorce me. I had become good at ignoring things.

Around that same time, LaShonda prophetically warned me that if I engaged in perverse conversations, that it would lead to extending my incarceration. Knowing through much experience that she too is a prophet of The Lord, I obeyed. At least for a while I did.

Some short while later, a younger professional I consistently visited in Maryland for the purpose of complete sex had reached out to me through a letter I received at the camp. He had learned I was in prison and so he reached out to me. I initially ignored him. But that wouldn't last long.

Simultaneously, I began to ignore and turn my back on LaShonda and even on my own daughter. I didn't want to call LaShonda because I would then be forced to talk about and confront my perverted actions, so I did not call. Jade, in turn, did not hear from me as well because I didn't have her telephone number in the prison TRULINCS system. This system allows inmates to communicate with people via text messaging, phone calls, and emails. Further, the only way I could talk to Jade was to go through LaShonda. So, I turned my back on them both. So, by way of electronic mail, LaShonda had to ask me to call on Easter Sunday 2021, and I consented.

In the summer of that same year, demons began to talk to me. I was convinced that it was GOD, but it actually was demons. These demons told me to discontinue calling and emailing everyone without any notice to them, and to only talk to LaShonda through email. So, I disappeared from everyone and entered into a journey with demons.

That July and for months following, I began to have very demonic exchanges and dialogue with familiar spirits. But I was convinced I was with The Lord. One evening, things shifted more demonically. I was in a trance of sorts, and I heard voices speaking to me, telling me things. I was certain it was GOD dealing with me. It is possible to serve the sins of lust and of the flesh, so much so that when demons begin to lead us, we have no idea it's even satanic. Sin is a deceiver. I had unknowingly entered a spiritual world, but it was not holy spiritual.

After spending many days alienating myself from those I love and who love me, later that July night, I stood at the sink in the bathroom while most of the inmates were asleep, and I literally left my body for what initially seemed to be 30 minutes or more. My spirit was somewhere else. Thinking back to that night, I believe witchcraft through demons was working on me. A spell and magic had captivated me.

That same night, I asked the presence, which I thought was GOD, to tell me what was happening, and its voice replied that I was climbing into the 'heavenlies.' And by the next morning, I became more prideful, being convinced that I was learning to move in the spiritual realm, between earth and the heavens. I was entirely convinced that GOD had given me a gift, a gift to travel in the spiritual realm, like a person having out-of-body experiences.

2 Corinthians 12:2 (KJV)

"I knew a man in Christ above fourteen years ago, (whether in the body, I cannot tell; or whether out of the body, I cannot tell: GOD knoweth;) such an one caught up to the third heaven."

Paul, in *2 Corinthians 12:2*, likely did have an out-of-body experience. Still, the devil can seemingly mimic what GOD does, as the magicians did in *Exodus Chapters 7 and 8*, with similar plagues manifested in Egypt.

When we err on the side of sin, we can eventually be made to believe that we are experiencing what is supernatural. And we are, but a supernatural event may or may not be from GOD. What was going on with me was completely demonic, and pride was the door that let it in.

The Devil Was My GOD

The homosexual community relates much of their movement to colors they stole from The Word of GOD, a holy multi-colored rainbow formed by GOD, and they perverted what GOD created. The rainbow symbolizes His promise to Noah and all of mankind. The devil attempted to steal this colorful arch. He even now thinks that he successfully stole it and that it belongs to him. Additionally, Satan has homosexuals calling themselves PRIDE, apparently insinuating that they are proud to be gay. Though The Bible explains how GOD feels about pride.

Proverbs 16:18 (KJV)

"Pride goeth before destruction, and an haughty spirit before a fall."

Pride comes before a fall. GOD hates, loathes, and detests a proud look.

Proverbs 6:16-19 (KJV)

[16] These six things doth the Lord hate: yea, seven are an abomination unto him:

[17] A proud look, a lying tongue, and hands that shed innocent blood,

[18] An heart that deviseth wicked imaginations, feet that be swift in running to mischief,

[19] A false witness that speaketh lies, and he that soweth discord among brethren.

Because He hates even the look of pride, obviously, His hatred for the action of pride is even more disgusting to GOD. There is nothing good about pride, nothing at all; nothing to boast about being prideful. Only the devil can make men love what GOD hates.

If you recall, I mentioned that Apostle Bismark had ministered to me through a prophetic Word of Wisdom and Knowledge in April 1998, calling out PRIDE. For me, the warfare of pride began long ago, but what had manifested by the summer of 2021 would only get worse.

Ultimately, pride is not a walk, talk, or gesture. In my estimation, pride equates to disobedience. Pride is you or me choosing to do what we want, choosing us over GOD, choosing our will instead of His. Pride essentially is disobedience, and disobedience is pride. The LGBTQ+ movement and community are nothing short of disobedience, disobedience through sexuality, and choosing self over what GOD originally intended for mankind.

A man did not name the LGBTQ+ community PRIDE. Satan himself named them PRIDE. Surely, it came out of the mouth of a man, woman, or committee. But the devil gave the name PRIDE to them, whether they knew it or not. Make no mistake about it.

So what happened was, I'd been distancing myself from people and began moving toward demons. I was becoming familiar with demons that had been so very familiar with me. These were familiar spirits *(Leviticus 19:31)*. For days and weeks, even into September, I would have these late-night encounters where I would wait to, I thought, hear from GOD in all sorts of visions and dreams. But none of it was GOD at all. None of it.

When I would exercise in the afternoons, I would see things. What I thought were angels and supernatural movements in the sky was demonic vision. And I'd feel like an energy or what I thought was the presence of GOD. But in all of this, I was actually under great demon deception and manipulation. And I was only able to be deceived in such an astounding way, because I had hardened my heart towards GOD. And I chose sin repeatedly over righteousness.

The devil had filled my space, and I had no idea. I would see, I thought demons and angels, assuming that this was an invitation by GOD into spiritual dimensions. I was even led to pray for faces. I'd see these faces in visions of people that I knew. Indeed, I was convinced this was all GOD. Why would demons tell me to pray for someone? But it was all a lie, further introducing me to demonic dimensions of great deception. It was not GOD listening to my prayers by then, so none of those prayers made any difference anyway. I was praying to demons. I had sold out repeatedly to the devil, so hell and its deceptions were now my god and guidance.

In *Matthew Chapter 4:1-11*, Satan was given access to Jesus' vision and hearing for a time, but Jesus was a holy man. But I had chosen evil and I was far from holy, so clearly, the devil had even more access to me, much more.

Around that same time, the guy I knew outside of prison, the aforementioned professional from Maryland, communicated again with me. Previously, I had ignored him and discarded his letter. Now, contact was made, and I called and emailed him. He almost immediately wanted to talk about the intimate times we had often shared years before. I agreed to these conversations briefly, but sin doesn't need long, not long at all. So, while I closed that door of conversation almost as quickly as I opened it, the door was still opened. And LaShonda's prophecy began to manifest, her prophecy of extended time in prison.

The prayers I prayed were demonic and prayers to devils. I was so deceived that I called family and friends again, after I felt GOD had released me to call them again. And I was bragging to some of them that I had been on an extended journey with GOD, which was why I had not been in touch with them. The devil had a plan, and that separation had been part of it.

A Suicidally Insane Prophet

Around October 2021, LaShonda told me I would receive documents related to a divorce in the mail. So, I began trying to court and woo her in back-to-back letters. I even wrote to Jade, telling her how much I loved and missed her. Then, after the papers arrived, I gave up on LaShonda, on us. That same night, I pleasured myself at least three times. However, sin is never satisfied. One door only leads to the next and the next.

A white guy, "Randall," had been in the shower some weeks prior, and when I had gotten out of the shower on one end, as I exited, he had his shower curtain open to show me his erection. I ignored him back then. But after I repeatedly pleased myself that night before, I stood in front of his cubicle. And I visibly flirted back at him. Shortly after that, we were in the showers. I went around the curtains to his shower, and we appeased one another. Randall had a huge reptile tattoo covering his back. And he had bragged previously to me about not ever going inside the chapel, as if he were anti-Christian. Soon after our lust-filled actions, I apologized to Randall and said that we could not do that again. I told him that GOD had convicted me. He did not seem bothered or phased by my statement. His demon spirit had already completed his assignment, and it did not care. I did not know at that time that other demons were lined up with their own assignments for me in the weeks and months to follow.

85

When I started my prison journey, I would typically sleep for six or seven hours a night. The lights typically turned out at 9 pm, and I fell asleep quite easily later each night. But during those nights when I believed I was climbing into heaven, I slept barely three or four hours a night. Much of it was due to "praying," but all of that soon turned into much anxiety throughout the days and nights. I felt, what now seems, bipolar at times. I would be thanking GOD one moment, and the next, I was very often overwhelmed with excessive depression. Demons were constantly at work in my thoughts. They were working overtime.

By then, I actually began to fear Bibles, and I refused to even have one in my cubicle. I was so confused at how I had just weeks prior been in a "glorious" trance and secret place with GOD. And now, I literally was losing my mind. I could not control it. I was losing it. And I decided that prescription medications were necessary to help me to sleep and to gain some control of my mind.

As this progressed, my prayer language, talking in tongues, did not help. I had been widely known online years before for having an in-depth, extraordinary prayer language **(Acts 2:4 and 2 Corinthians 12:28, 30).** Tongue-talking videos of me went viral in 2019. So, as my mind was slipping, I ran to prayer and tongues, but it still did not help. The demons in my "trances" before were with me now, too. But this time, they were manifesting their ultimate intent, to drive me crazy. And they soon became unmerciful towards me, with increasingly wicked dreams, violently pushing me as I lay in the bed. From November into

December 2021, I was speedily mentally collapsing ever so quickly.

On Thanksgiving Day, I was suddenly extremely depressed. And as November concluded, I increasingly withdrew from other inmates into mid-December. I could barely sleep. I did not shower much. I did not work out anymore. Lifting weights and cardio had, until then, been a very regular part of my routine for many months. But by then, my food consumption had greatly decreased, so I was losing weight, too. I just wanted to lie down constantly, be lethargic, and be lazy. I didn't want to do anything. I felt worn out. I was spiraling down.

What also helped me to unfold mentally was that LaShonda had told me that she was referred to as a villain for divorcing me. She was criticized by others for the decision she had made, she told me. So, she told me that she told people, even religious church people, why it was that she was divorcing me. That she was divorcing me because I had cheated on her. That revelation took me even further downhill psychologically. Because I understood that people would now know that I was not only in prison and that I had cheated, but that it had been with males. So, I lost even more control over my mind at these impeding and intrusive thoughts.

As Christmas day approached, I began emailing almost everyone on my list. Emails strongly suggested that I was falling apart in my mind, that I needed medication, and that I desperately needed help. I even emailed the warden and other prison staff, crying out for help. At one point, at the computer, I passed out right there. After regaining consciousness, I got up, began walking, and ended up sitting on the bed in a cubicle that was not even my own. I was losing my mind rapidly.

During those times, not being able to sleep much at all, I would sit in the TV room at all hours of the night and day. One day, without thought, I shockingly began to rub the back of my head up against the wall. I was convinced that I needed medicinal help in order to rest and get away from thoughts of deep sadness, anguish, depression, and now seemingly suicide.

Following those alerting emails to family and friends, as well as to the warden and medical staff, I was prescribed buspirone by the medical staff. Buspirone is the same medication that was taken by the guy I quarantined with only 15 months prior. He was suicidal, too. I was now thinking like him and taking the same medication as him.

Sex is not just sex; it is a transference. There was never "completed sex" with him, not even close. But no matter the act, the moment your spirit opens up, demons can enter into you, as they did me. Whether you have a masturbating partner, even just on the phone, demons can transfer. What was on him and in him was now fully manifesting through me. It took over a year, but it manifested, and that was not even the tip of the iceberg that was about to melt.

The buspirone I was prescribed was not working as quickly as I felt it should, and I was obviously losing more control of my thoughts. So, on the evening of Tuesday, December 21, 2021, I was willingly admitted to the suicide watch across the street from the camp, at the Federal Corrections Institution (FCI) prison there in Ashland. This location was the same place I had quarantined in over a year before.

Later that evening, under the supervision of one inmate at a time who all worked shifts, I was now wearing a smock and lying on a plastic-covered mat on a metal bed in a very small room. This miniature room included a toilet connected to a sink and a ceiling light that generally never went out.

As I remained there that night, I walked around the tiny room praising GOD and even testifying to one interested inmate who watched me on the other side of a plastic door, not glass.

There had been two inmates by then who had watched me during their separate shifts. But around midnight, the second inmate ended his shift, and another one showed up to relieve him. It was a black guy, maybe in his forties. As he sat in the chair looking forward, I lay in bed facing the opposite wall away from him. And without thought, I suddenly began to touch myself. So, while maybe one hour ago, I had been praising GOD, I thought, now I was with my hand under the smock, touching myself. Though he could not see my hand or private parts, I am sure the inmate was in total shock.

Once it seemed that he wouldn't respond to my actions, I stood up and asked him if it was okay if I masturbated on the side by the toilet, outside of his immediate view. He replied that it would not be a good idea. Little did I know that I had just committed PREA. What did PREA mean anyway? Technically it stands for the Prison Rape Elimination Act (PREA). It was signed into law in 2003 and is meant to deter sexual assault in prison. It's when an inmate acts in a sexual way and or makes sexual comments towards another inmate.

When you constantly agree to sin, it will take you down roads you never knew existed. You will eventually find yourself doing what you never thought you would. By this time, I was not touching myself on my own and of my own intent. The homosexual demons I had been serving were now controlling my actions and hand. In my own mind, I knew I had done and said something deeply frowned upon by the prison, but I was no longer in my right mind. I literally had lost control.

Because of my actions and statement, inmates could no longer supervise me on suicide watch. I had to now be watched by prison guards. I was in deep trouble, and it happened so quickly. I had lost control.

CHAPTER 6
DESPERATION AND DESTRUCTION

Repeated Self-Mutilations

A few days later, after my actions, it was a Thursday and I had lyingly convinced one or two of the psychologists that I was no longer suicidal.

After I lied, instead of redressing in the gray clothes that I wore when I arrived at suicide watch, I was told to dress in orange attire. For the place where they were taking me, orange attire was the standard. As they prepared to take me not far from where I was already, I was handcuffed for the first time in my life. At the camp, inmates never had to wear handcuffs. I had never worn them before. But being transported to this new unit, you had to enter in handcuffs. I was then led to the SHU (Special/Segregated Housing Unit), also known by prisoners as the Hole.

Inmates can end up in the SHU for anything from fighting to having drugs on them or for drugs being detected in their urine. I soon understood that they put me there because of being sexual in front of an inmate. I did not know what the end result would be, but for the first time while incarcerated, I was in trouble, while in trouble.

The Hole (or SHU) was a type of hell. Being there actually felt like a bottomless pit, a hole.

When I first arrived, one person was in the cell with me, and the others right next to us were in the same very small cells, normally 7 feet by 11 feet. They are most often described as small enough to make pacing difficult, which is true. The cell included a set of narrow and uncomfortable bunk beds, a miniature sink directly connected to a cold and damp toilet, a small stool attached to the very hard metal floor that looked to have been put there 60 years ago, and a small floor-attached table. The cells are dark, dreary, and tight, very tight.

The camp seemed to be maybe 20 years old. The SHU was often very loud, with bars for doors all around. This was my first time behind actual bars—we had no bars in quarantine. The glaring ceiling lights were on from 6 am until about 9 pm. The lights were even like a punishment, making complete rest and total peace impossible.

Demonic things began to occur almost immediately. My roommate was from the camp like me, and he wanted to talk a lot, and I would listen. This decreased the time to be consumed by my speedily failing mind. While I knew that what I had done in front of the inmate about two days before was wrong by prison standards, I was still initially optimistic. I thought I would only be there for a short while and then go back to the camp. Yet, I'd been deceived by myself, not knowing where those PREA-related actions and comments would lead me. But the devil had much more planned than a PREA.

One night, as I lay in the top bunk, unable to sleep, I worshiped GOD. But as a punishment and to make me afraid of talking to GOD, a demon's presence literally sat on my chest. It felt as if my chest was on fire. My chest and orange t-shirt were both soon soaking wet. I was in total shock at how the enemy was given access to my body and the torment that followed. So, I soon became afraid to pray and reach out to GOD.

With each day came more and more torment and demonic ideas and thoughts, spiritual and natural torment. All day, I opened and closed my eyes to excessive lighting while listening to loud inmates who were restricted to tight spaces just like I was. I barely ever slept. And I was in total torment when it was quieter, such as late at night. I wanted the inmates talking to help keep me distracted from the demons within and around me. But there was a bigger picture at play. Lights and inmates were a small piece of what was happening to me. They were natural. But my mind was falling into hell and constantly in torment.

One night, once my cell roommate, or "cellie" as we called them, had fallen asleep, I took my wrist and rubbed it up against the sharp, pointy-edged fire extinguisher in the room. But it hurt too bad, and I knew cutting it would be too painful, so I stopped. Around the same time, I looked at a COVID–19 face mask and a plastic bag, and the devil gave me the idea to suffocate myself, to wear the mask and tie the bag around my head. But I refused to do so.

That Christmas week of 2021, not being able to sleep, the devil put in my mind a scripture I remembered to be located towards the end of the book of Deuteronomy. Once he locked the scripture passage in my mind, I could not help but keep thinking about that verse: *Deuteronomy 32:30* paraphrased, "One can chase a thousand, and two can put ten thousand to flight." I was suddenly obsessed with finding and reading it. But before I could find it, the devil put the whole reason for the memory right before my eyes.

Frantically searching the latter chapters of the book of Deuteronomy, I then looked upon chapter 28 and verse number 34. This is the moment when the devil read The Bible to me, giving me his interpretation of the verse. He read to me from The Bible, as he did to Jesus in *Matthew Chapter 4:6*. This written warning was a prophecy in verse 34, along with other warnings, directed towards those who had decided to disobey and rebel against GOD continually. It is promised as part of a curse to those who, as I had, made a commitment to be rebellious and disobedient to GOD and His Word. Verse 34 promised that this rebel would eventually look at themselves–e.g., in the mirror–and realize that they have gone mad/insane/crazy. Specifically, *Deuteronomy 28:34* reads: "So that thou shalt be mad for the sight of thine eyes which thou shalt see."

I was in complete shock to read this, quickly shutting The Bible. The devil began to convince me that I would go completely mad. And it was already happening because when I continually chose to serve the devil, and not GOD, demons and devils would be allowed to have their way with me, even to the point of bringing

94

to pass a warning in The Bible that could become my literal manifestation. I immediately became even more afraid to read The Bible. I felt tormented by The Word of GOD. The devil's prophecy on my life was coming to pass viciously, forcefully, and quickly.

Subsequently, on my mother's birthday, Tuesday, December 28th, 2021, in the early morning hours, the devil spoke to me. As I lay in the top bunk bed and my cellie slept below, I heard him tell me to walk. The ceiling was very low in the SHU, so my feet could easily reach and rest on the ceiling as I lay on the bed on my back. As I lay there, eyes on the ceiling, a demon said, "Walk." Not even considering the outcome, my body obeyed the god it had served over and over and over again. I walked with my back on the bed and feet on the ceiling. My body then crashed to the floor. The prison staff came running to my aid. And I lied, saying it was an accident, but my cellie knew better. I was then escorted back to the cell, the fall resulting in pain in one elbow and a foot.

Then, that same evening, as my cellie talked to other inmates at our cell bars, I began to feel completely out of control and under the dominance of a supernatural entity, a strong, great demon. And without warning to my cellie, who was looking in the opposite direction, I climbed down from the top bunk, stood on the floor, and observed a point of contact (between the beds), a contact to end my life. And I forcefully and with great vengeance violently smashed my forehead against the sharp metal-edged corner that joins the top and bottom beds. I did this with so much strength and might that right after the collision, I bounced back and fell to the floor. My forehead was split open, and blood was pouring out of me and onto my clothing and the floor. The next thing I knew, the lieutenant on duty was there and saying something about his fear of coming into contact with my blood. But he and other staff still helped me as much as they could. I was then pulled on a sheet by a few staff members through the hallway, in front of the other SHU cell inmates, and then hauled into an ambulance.

On the way to the hospital, I pretended to be unresponsive, trying to make them think I was even worse off. I did that until I was given smelling salt. After that, I had no choice but to act coherently.

As we rode to the hospital, I could feel a demon's presence as if groaning and growling heavily within my chest. This demon was so very restless. I could tell it wanted to manifest even more.

The paramedics questioned me as we were en route to the local emergency room. They also wanted to confirm that my cellie had not done this to me. I told them that it was an accident. Soon, we arrived at the hospital. And I lay handcuffed to the bed with prison guards watching over me as I was tended to by a male doctor.

I even recall demons directing me to take the doctor's scissors and to stab him with it. Thankfully, I had the power not to obey that command. Once my forehead was stitched up and I was given a tetanus shot, I was transported back to the prison and back to suicide watch, where hell and its vengeance were waiting to attack me even the more.

Approximately a day or two later, I was lying once again on the mattress-covered metal bed, this time facing the door and being watched by a prison guard. I then looked to my left, and a dark shadow stood there. Then it vanished and suddenly reappeared, standing just behind me. This dark entity then touched my right shoulder and disappeared again. And suddenly, I heard it talking from inside of my body. It began to tell me that I was not alone as I heard various other voices inside me too. And the more these demons interacted with my mind, the crazier I became.

On Friday, December 31, 2021, I asked the lieutenant who regularly visited me on his night shift, I asked him to chain me to the bed. I was convinced that I would hurt myself. But he abruptly said no. He told me it was nearly New Year's, insinuating that being in chains at such a time would be a horrible situation. I guess he didn't want me to start the first day of the New Year in chains.

Soon after, I began to see, through a vision, wolves hiding in trees, like in a dark forest. And I kept hearing Satan tell me to worship him. I would try not to worship him, but eventually, I would, literally. I also began to both hear and feel bombs going off right next to me. I was constantly terrified. As the bombs went off, I thought to get on the floor to hide from them, but Satan showed me a row of bombs waiting on the floor, so I fearfully stayed in bed. And the more I would not worship him, the more he attacked me, attacked me in my thoughts and my body.

Very soon, I was taking 50 mg of Trazodone and 50 mg of Prozac, which was quickly increased to 100 mg of each of them. Trazodone is supposed to aid sleep, but even with 100 mg, I only slept maybe 1 hour total during each 24-hour period. And when I did sleep, hell and demons were waiting on me with nightmares of sorrow, rejection, fear, worry, anxiety, perversion, lust, and homosexuality. All of my rest and sleep were inundated and filled with the power and vision of demons constantly. Demons were now ruling everything about me.

Trapped In A Horror Show

As I remained on suicide watch, the prison staff was obviously upset with me. They had to watch me while often working overtime when they were already short-staffed. I was also being seen by all three psychologists on staff at FCI Ashland. They each came to see me regularly. They were attempting to get me well enough to be discharged from suicide watch. Even the chief psychologist spent much time working with me. However, none of it helped because they only used natural means and methods.

The chief psych encouraged me to meet all the goals necessary to get out of suicide watch. They wanted to transition me to the next phase, to another prison, for more help. But I felt they were not concerned with my well-being whatsoever. I believe they merely wanted me out of their hands. I was taking up too much of their precious time, I thought. One of the psychologists would get very visibly angry with me. Another one became furious when I chose not to write down a list of things to live for. I was non-compliant, and it upset them. It gave them the idea that I did not want their help. But I was too mentally ill to even understand that I needed their help.

The chief psychologist would try and focus me on books I could read to help me get better. Initially, I couldn't have a book in the suicidal watch room with me. I guess they thought I could hurt myself with it. I hated one book because it actually talked about demons on a boat, and I didn't want to read about the things that were fighting me. Eventually, I did want the prison staff to think that I was getting better so I could get out of there. So, I would put the books beside me on the bed, pretending to read them.

Once, as a book of theirs lay next to me, a demon gave me a vision of a cloud under one sentence on the book's front cover. The sentence said something about yielding, and I took it to mean yielding to Satan. I was sure Satan had total access to my mind, eyes, ears, and feelings. Nothing seemingly was off limits to him. I was sure either Satan could read my mind or at least plant thoughts so well that it was as if they were my own thoughts.

As time went on, things got even more strangely demonic. As I lay in bed, demons wanted to convince me that they had power over my limbs and bodily faculties. On the bed and wearing a smock, my index finger, all on its own, tapped so very quickly on the plastic mat. Just as Satan forced me to smash my head into the edged metal, this was a reminder to me that demons ruled my body, my fingers. It was as if I were watching a horror movie, my own horror movie, where I was the star and things unnaturally moved on their own, and things began to appear and disappear on their own. It felt like I was in episodes of The Twilight Zone or Tales from the Darkside, except it wasn't on a big TV flatscreen or at an AMC Theatre. Instead, it was all inside of me.

Demons brought to my mind a song Elbernita (Twinkie) Clark sings: "Accept What GOD Allows." I began to consider giving in to this madness. All of this was to try to bring me to submit to Satan.

As these demon powers increased their tenacity, willpower, and determination, I lay in bed one night, and I felt an object in my throat. I literally felt it crawling up through my throat. Demons were intruding into every area of my body. I felt physically manipulated, traumatized, terrorized, and spellbound. I lacked power over them. I thought of a horror movie I'd watched years ago, where an entity's hand was crawling up through the throat of a person. Satan was telling me that he was coming to take control, to own me, and overpower me.

I lived day and night in shock at all of this. Then, what was in my throat was no longer there. It had reached the inside of my mouth. Horrified, I walked over to the metal toilet and took out what appeared to be hardened tiny plastic. Afraid, I didn't want to inspect or look at it further. I quickly flushed it down the toilet.

Like Lightning Hitting My Mind

Trying to comply with the chief psychologist's directives, even though I was still losing my mind, I was discharged from the suicide watch for the second time and went back to the SHU. I had told them I was no longer suicidal. I told them what they wanted to hear. This would have been on or around Friday,

January 7, 2022, when the discharge from suicide watch back to the SHU occurred.

Inmates can't normally access the commissary to shop for food and other things in the SHU. Shopping is very limited in the SHU. So, people tend to lose weight quickly there because the three served meals are not often very filling for a full 24-hour period. We weren't even allowed to purchase our own deodorant or toothpaste, and the staff can be stingy with the very basic kind they gave us. So, we sparingly used the little they did give us. Colgate or Crest would be a dream in the SHU. Their deodorant was often liquid in a tiny plastic pouch that barely did the job, if at all. You're meant to suffer and loathe the SHU experience so that you don't get in trouble and return.

Upon returning to the SHU, I was put in a cell with another guy from the camp. I will refer to him as "Travis." I had met Travis the prior summer in the chapel at the camp. By then, he'd been there in the SHU for around seven months. Travis looked very skeletal and frail. At first, I did not recognize him. And I observed nearly immediately that he had a severe case of OCD (obsessive-compulsive disorder).

Travis was awaiting designation to another prison as they were completing an investigation to see if the prison could find him guilty of directing people outside the camp to bring contraband there and throw it over the fence. They believed he likely helped orchestrate these things. So, while I was forced to observe him clean and clean, he soon began talking about having ongoing conversations with his deceased grandmother. Travis also had a

Bible lying on the floor at the bottom of the bed, and he would read it daily, though I could tell he was going mad himself.

People may not realize this, but being in such a small space for a long time can have a horrible effect on people's psyches. Further, most guys spend a month or two in the SHU, not half a year. However, being under investigation can easily extend anyone's time there, as happened to Travis. So day in and day out, I would watch him constantly clean the cell bars and other parts of the 7 by 11 cell. Being in that small space for so long seemed to be ruining his mind. He was declining mentally, and as I observed him going crazy, so was I.

The first day or two (I was required to take the bottom bed since I had been suicidal), I felt something peel off my face like a mask had been pulled roughly and violently from my face. This signaled to me that something within me was trying to manifest, like a transformation was attempting to happen. And actually, a change was happening.

Around this same time, I had had no bowel movement for a week, which was partly due to constant laying around and the meds I was taking, but I also believe it was demonically related. After all, he was controlling other parts of my body, too. After I was put back in the SHU, a SHU nurse gave me a large bottle of magnesium citrate. The magnesium citrate tasted like soda water with a fruit-like scent. I drank this while in the SHU cell with Travis. Very soon, I had many bowel movements in the small cell, lacking ventilation. The movements lasted for one and a half days.

While there, Travis remembered me ministering to him the previous summer at the camp chapel. He even said I ministered to him with accuracy. So, watching me constantly lay around, he encouraged me to return to GOD.

By then, I was in no position to minister. Day and night, I would lay there with my eyes wide open, especially at night. I hated the sounds of the guards doing their hourly rounds. The sound of the doors slamming as they entered and exited the SHU unit felt like further traumatization. Doors constantly shutting felt like lightning hitting my mind.

With me going out of my mind, there was so much against me. Sleep, peace, and rest were alienated from me. I was isolated, with no family–to call or at least being too crazy to do so–no friends, and feeling reprobate and all alone. Even GOD had left me. So I was in a small space, changing into something or someone else I did not recognize. I would just lay there, believing GOD had entirely left me. Being too afraid of the devil's punishment to worship GOD, I didn't dare to worship GOD. So I just lay in silence for hours and hours for days and days.

Tempted To Drug Myself To Death

Watching Travis' OCD helped me to go mad, too. But relief came late Sunday, January 9, 2022. After I was moved, I was transferred to a cell with "Tommy."

Tommy was tall and very overweight, and I had shared some inspiration with him at the camp a few months back. But by this time, I had become someone else. I was becoming what was underneath the mask.

The night Tommy arrived, he had returned from the hospital for having accidentally removed a toenail while cutting them, and he had bled a lot. He was known at the camp to be clumsy. So he was brought to the SHU around 1 am that night as they were determining if he did it on purpose. I took the top bunk, and he took the bottom bunk as he was very obese.

I was so thankful to be away from OCD Travis.

Before leaving us together, the guard said he knew Tommy and I would get along, likely because of our very recent history of hurting ourselves. No decent human with any amount of sympathy would have said that to me or anyone. It seemed demons wouldn't stop using people to talk to me. But this was only the beginning of me hearing from demons through people.

It was in there with Tommy that the nightmares intensified. I would wake up all through the night. The dreams were horrifying. In some of these, I was in tight spaces with demons or images of horrifying demon faces that sought to fill me with fear. When I could sleep, I would often wake up extremely terrified. Demon spirits created, produced, and streamed these dreams to my scared mind. I was afraid to sleep. I got no rest, and the devil even read to my mind the scripture: "There is no rest/peace for the wicked" *(Isaiah 48:22)*.

Tommy was on many medications, and he was likely soon to go home on Compassionate Care release or the Cares Act. Due to COVID-19, inmates were getting early releases for medically related reasons. One of the medications he took was Nitrogen. He had told me that if he took too much, it could kill him. I even

104

wondered why they would put me in a room with easy reach to this sort of medication, given my recent history.

One night, as I couldn't sleep, Tommy slept. And I got off the top bunk bed, held the Nitrogen bottle, and read it. The devil told me to take the whole bottle. Demons would challenge me to do what they told me. These demons were further angered when I did not adhere to their demands. But I knew not to take them because what if they didn't kill me and the whole purpose was to escape life, so I thought.

While food was not plentiful in the SHU, this worked out for me because I was afraid to get constipated again and possibly have reintroduced sciatica issues. I'd suffered from sciatica before going to prison, which for me was related to constipation, so I didn't want to eat a lot anyway. The paperwork that came with the psych meds said that they could cause constipation. So, by then I had stopped taking Prozac and Trazodone. The prescription details also said both pills could lead to suicidal thoughts. So, when the nurses came to give me meds daily, I would refuse by this time.

In suicide watch, I saw psych staff daily, but as soon as I was in the SHU, they came maybe once a week. It was even more clear that they wanted me out of that prison, out of their sight and off of their agenda and schedule.

Having nothing else to do, I often stared at Tommy as he slept. One night, around 2 am, it looked like Tommy had died. He had gone still. Getting proper care in that isolated environment is impossible, especially if you have an emergency. That night,

Tommy lay there, very still, like he'd had a heart attack and died. So, I hurried over to the cell bars and called for the guards. They rushed and aided him. Soon after, he was better, and I was then put back in the cell with him. One rule was for certain: Inmates cannot be in cells alone. This is to make it impossible for uninterrupted suicide. We were eyes and ears for one another.

The state I was in mentally had me very twisted. I was so mentally depraved then that I even hated showering, so my body often stank. But when I did agree to shower, I had to leave the cell and go to another floor where the showers were. So, I rarely showered often for the embarrassment and hatred of having to wear handcuffs in order to leave the cell to go shower. In the SHU, you cannot leave the cell without handcuffs on. So, I would shower once a week or less.

After about ten days with Tommy, he was sent back to the camp to be released home soon, I expected. I envied him for that. Before he left, Tommy, who was supposedly a Christian, oddly and strangely said to me as he exited the cell that I could hang myself with a sheet if it got too bad. Then he said he was joking.

Almost immediately, I was moved back to the cell where OCD Travis was.

CHAPTER 7
BECOMING THE DARKNESS

Becoming The Darkness

In the SHU, inmates from the prison are to be in cells with inmates from the prison, and the same goes for those from the camp. That is why I had been placed with both Travis and Tommy.

While I was in the cell with Tommy, the guy I'd been intimate with in the shower the prior fall, Randall, had just been the cellmate with Travis. Randall had to go to the hospital earlier that day. Inmates must go to the SHU the night before being transported to the hospital. So I was now in the upper bunk Randall had just slept in the night before.

Realizing that the person who played a massive role in my downward spiral had been in the bed I now slept in blew my mind. I was certain at that time that this was planned by the devil. By this time, I determined the devil had set everything up, even if it was just a coincidence.

Things only progressed for the worse from there. On about Thursday, January 20, 2022, demons began to interact with me in greater, more heart-pounding ways. I had dreams of another guy from the camp who was visibly similar to Travis. In these tormented dreams, I and this other guy were in what seemed to be a boxing ring. We were opponents and supposed to fight. These nightmares convinced me that Travis and I were the perfect storm in that cell together and that I was going to have no choice but to fight him.

As if that weren't crazy enough, I would have thoughts, and Travis would suddenly talk about them. For instance, out of nowhere, I became obsessed with thinking about some episode of a television program I'd watched decades before. Suddenly, Travis began to talk about the details of that exact episode. It was as if I were literally trapped in unending madness, and the actors at the time were now me and Travis.

I just couldn't see how the devil could read my mind. Or how he had planted the thought in me and then directed Travis to speak my thoughts out loud. My mind would constantly race nonstop, from thought to thought, memory to memory. I could control none of this at all. Oddly, I would also see cast members' faces from programs I'd watched years ago. Then, I would become obsessed with remembering the program's name and its actors' screen names, but I could not recall. Then I would hear Satan whisper to me the name of the show and the actors in it. I could recognize the voice to be Satan or his demon. None of this made any sense then, but what I was sure of was that Satan now owned my whole thought life. I had become his. Unrepented nonstop sin made me his.

With each passing day, the devil's control over my mind and body advanced and multiplied. In one of the most horrifying dreams at that time, demons kept predicting to me that I would get worse. They would give me their own foretelling demonic timelines. And they were proven right.

When Satan becomes your lord, when you habitually practice sin, he can eventually own your future, and he can accurately tell you what is going to occur. This can also be how today's psychics and mediums receive their ability to foretell accurately.

In one demon-spirited dream, I was driving in the pitch dark to where I'd lived from the 5th grade till I had graduated and gone away to electronics school. The address was 1944 Chris Drive. In this dream, I was in front of the split foyer house. Darkness was all around me; it was a great, gross, and consuming darkness. However, I could see even blacker trees in the distance and hear birds chirping loudly in those trees. It was the most haunting chirping one could ever imagine. In this particular nightmare, standing near the car, I shot an invisible machine gun in my hands at the birds in the trees that I could hear but not see. My hands actually formed and were the gun. I was trying to shoot and fight and conquer this darkness that was attempting to rule my life and mind. In the dream, right before I woke up, I had the "gun" in my hand, and I kept on turning around in circles and shooting rapidly and repeatedly. But soon, I could shoot and fight no more. Then, I transformed into the deep darkness that surrounded me. I could no longer fight it, so I became it. This dream was a demon's prediction to me and would soon come to pass.

As this Twilight Zone continued, a guard walked past our cell on Sunday, January 30, 2022. He was singing some song referencing that nightmare I'd just had. The enemy used anyone he could to get to me. It was hell on earth, hell in my mind, hell inside of me, and I knew it. No one was off limits, not even the prison guards.

Demon voices in my head also told me that my ministry and I were phony and not real. He told me that it was all a lie and that it was him who actually said: "I will deliver you." I understand now that even some "prophetic" dreams I had while at the camp were indeed an implant of Satan. Some were the devil's "prophecies." This demon was aggressively convincing me that the only one who ever spoke to me and that I trusted in was indeed Satan, all of the time.

Unholy living can easily lead to deception. The more we serve sin, the more Satan can talk to us. Every voice is not GOD. And the only way to discern and avoid deception is to turn to GOD wholeheartedly. The unrepented sin that we continue to practice can eventually make Satan and his deceptions our god.

With little sleep, the nightmares I had were becoming more and more wicked and wild. In one, I was wrapped up like a mummy and driven down a dark hill in the back of a hurst inside a coffin. In another, I was at a church pissing in a chair. While in another, I'd be vomiting up oatmeal, with the idea that the devil was coming out of me, only to wake up still spiritually bound. In another, nude and lewd men stood behind bars. While in another,

I was in a hot tub for seemingly hours, unable to move or speak. My dreams were a complete torment, from one torment to the next.

In that cell with Travis, I continued to deteriorate. I was literally peeing in milk cartons because I didn't want to leave the top bunk, though the toilet was only a few steps away. I was drinking water from my vitamin bottles, which I stored on the top bunk because I didn't want to walk to the sink much, if at all.

Around Wednesday, February 2, 2022, demons entered me even more. And they used other people even more. A guy in the cell next to me and Travis suddenly began talking about two guys being alone together on an island and having to eat one another to survive. This chatter added to the violent narrative Satan had locked in my mind of having to fight Travis. On one hand, I thought, of course, I would never do such a heinous act. But then I kept remembering how I forcefully and violently smashed my head over a month prior. That seemed to tell me the truth. I was so afraid, even of myself. It wouldn't be long now before the transformation was complete.

Somebody Was About To Get Hurt

The coveted words in the SHU to many were: "You've been designated." These words mean inmates' days were numbered, and they could expect to leave soon and be transported to another federal correctional institution (FCI), no longer having to live in such a place as the SHU.

Because of the PREA, I couldn't go back to the camp, and I could not stay at the Ashland FCI either, where the inmate I committed the act in front of was still incarcerated. Further, I loathed the idea of being shipped to where I had no idea I was going. So, on or about Thursday, February 3, 2022, the warden came through the SHU and said: "Trumbo, you've been designated." My heart immediately sank. I could not fathom in the mental state I was in, being transitioned elsewhere.

A few weeks before this announcement, I heard one officer say to another that I'd be killed at a low. By 'low' he meant in a prison other than a camp. FCI Ashland was a: low. There are prison levels: camps for people with minimum security points, as I started with, are the lowest level. Then, there are low, medium, high, and so forth. While I was technically at a low by this time there at the FCI, I was not in the general population. I was in the SHU, so all I had known was a camp up until then.

What some guards and inmates said in my hearing about other prisons astounded me and made me more afraid of what was coming. In addition, being transported elsewhere meant wearing handcuffs, which I was still not accustomed to. So, just the idea of riding on a bus or plane in handcuffs for long periods of time, that thought further terrified me. So, with the warden's loud announcement, things went from worse to much, much worse.

In the movie "Fallen," starring Denzel Washington, demons leap from person to person through touch. But no touching was needed in my situation. Demons were jumping from person to person while also growing inside of me. One day, I got off the top bed to use the toilet. Travis was lying down, and I looked at him, and I uncontrollably softly growled. It was like a wild animal, dog, or wolf growling from inside me at Travis. It was not loud enough for him to hear, but I sure heard and felt it. It was only about to get worse. Somebody was about to get hurt.

On or around Friday, February 4, 2022, Travis, my cellie, played chess with another SHU inmate as I lay quietly in the top bunk. Of course, they were in separate cells, so they told each other about their game movements, which is how it's played in the SHU. So, to further fill my mind with death and murder, the conversation between the two of them abruptly shifted to talking about killing the bishop, a chess game piece.

Then suddenly, another inmate in the other cell right next to us started saying: "Kill the M**F**." His voice sounded wicked and full of hate and hostility. I understood that Satan was further giving me the idea that Travis and I would soon fight each other in that cell. I envisioned it as a blood bath. Whether two guys on an island, a chess piece, or through the mouth of the guy in the cell right next to us, Satan wanted me consumed with the idea that I would soon and, without choice, start a fight with Travis.

On Saturday, February 5, 2022, the dream of me shooting an invisible gun, turning into the surrounding darkness, and fully becoming the entity under the mask began manifesting. Lying in the bed, my hand balled into a fist all on its own. The enemy kept pushing me to fight Travis. As I continued lying in the top bunk bed, something inside of me then tried to raise me off of the bed. I was being forced to get up. I was under attack from something living inside of me. So, I hurriedly began to hold the bars tight to avoid doing something appalling and insane.

The incident on Tuesday, December 28, 2021, where Satan had me 'walk' and I fell out of bed, was happening all over again. But this time, the demons within me wanted to manifest and include another inmate. I just knew that if it started, it would end in much blood and likely death. When two inmates are locked in a cell together as we were, a fight can normally only be interrupted if we were handcuffed by guards, and I knew it would never make it to that point. The devil wanted me to try and Kill the M**F**! It was either 'fight or run!' And I was looking for a way to run.

Because I refused to fight Travis, demons directed me to ask a passing female guard for a pencil so that I could write a "cop out" – a form inmates fill out to get assistance from various prison staff. He wanted me to write it to the warden and other staff. Satan wanted me to tell them that they were all chomos–a prison term for child molesters. And that they were homosexuals. The devil wanted me to kill me or try to make the staff angry enough to kill me. Satan wanted me dead.

If the devil is after your life; if anyone reading this knows the devil is trying to kill you, you must realize that it's only because a great purpose and call from The Lord is in your life! Whatever you do, make a decision now to stay alive!

By this point, my mind was under total siege, as Satan now tried to have me lie and tell other inmates in the cells next to us that I was a child molester. I was convinced I'd eventually give in to his demands and either fight or lie about myself and others. My permanently scarred forehead from what I'd done to myself in late December was evidence that I would soon submit to Satan again; that I'd become the darkness. I had become increasingly fearful of the demons living inside of me. Something inside of me was attacking me! Somebody was about to get hurt!

I Could Fight Back No More

As I continued to struggle with Satan on Saturday, February 5, 2022, Satan drove my mind downward more.

As the same female guard did her rounds–checking on all of us, I then told her that I was the one who had been previously on suicide watch, and I said to her: "I feel dangerous." So, for the third time, I returned to suicide watch. Once back there, other inmates watched me again from the other side of the door. Shortly after arriving there, I kept rubbing the top of my head until, unusually, much of my hair fell out all over the plastic-covered mattress. One staff member told me to stop before I had no hair left, but I kept on. I did this for many hours.

This event was connected, I was sure, with the devil's prophecy of becoming mad and becoming the darkness. After I looked down at my hair on the mattress, Satan told me that I was like Sampson now and that I had no strength left to fight him *(Judges 16:1-21).* With that realization and understanding, I stood up and went to the inmate watching over me from the other side of the door. And as I was wearing the smock, I began to piss on the floor from inside the smock, all while telling the inmate lies about myself and others. I could fight back no more. Much of my hair was gone, and so was my strength against all of this.

Like when I bashed my head, this event was sudden and without hesitation. I just got up, and began to piss on the floor. I also began to lie while using every bit of profanity I could think of. I told lies about my wife, lies about inmates at the camp, all right there in front of the inmate who looked to be in his late twenties. I then danced around in the piss, chanting and writing with my spit on my index finger onto the metal wall. I wrote hateful statements against the warden, against GOD, and The Church. The words could barely be deciphered, but I refused to disobey the demands coming from within any longer.

I eventually hit my head on the wall, and that is when the inmate finally called an officer, and they rushed to me. The prison staff wanted to come in, but the protocol was that I had to be cuffed for them to enter, and I refused to do so. They pleaded with me for seemingly hours. So eventually, they pepper-sprayed me so that I could be subdued. My piss on the floor, saliva on the metal wall, food strewn on the floor, my blood on the wall, and me soon laying on the floor, having been pepper sprayed. It stung my body, but I was so madly insane that it had not registered much at all.

After that episode, I was taken to a shower in the SHU area and told to shower to get the pepper spray off of my body. I then obeyed their directives.

While in the shower, I saw what the devil had promised me. On some metal siding in the shower, I tried not to look, but I saw my reflection briefly. I saw a "mad" man, just as Satan had assured me I would.

Things just seemed to go upside down even the more. Demons raged inside of me. Around those same dates, but not recalling

116

some details, I was chained to the bed because I had been fighting back at the officers. Several chains were wrapped around my chest, attaching me to the bed. I seemed to be in and out of demonic trances by then. I couldn't sleep. I was trapped in what very apparently was the realm of the demonic.

While chained to the bed, a guard came to relieve another guard. Apparently because of the urinating incident in front of a working inmate and being so out of control, I was watched by prison staff again. But it was not just a guard this time. It was wearing a black hood. Its eyes were blue and snake-like. It never even made eye contact with me, never spoke. Rather, while chained to the bed, as I turned my head to inspect it more carefully, it looked beyond me, beyond the walls, as if it was seeing the demon spirits huddled all around me.

I still barely slept. By this time again, I was likely usually taking 100 mg of Trazodone again, but I still very barely slept. But when this hooded guard arrived, I was soon asleep. When I woke up, it was gone, and I became even worse off. I'm sure it had put me to sleep and had cast further spells on me. I was in hell. Consumed with hell.

I Drank Toilet Water, Seven Times

I stayed in chains for maybe a day or more. I don't remember. Eventually, the chains were removed, and in their stead, I wore a "box." This contraption gives you some freedom, and a person can move around more. But I was still cuffed with chains around my waist, both attached to a box under the front of my waist.

Once, while I was lying down and wearing the "box," medical and corrections staff came in. One of the guards was recording with a device. They were there to take my temperature. At this temperature check, the physician's assistant shook very uncontrollably. She shook so much that she soon fidgeted and dropped the temperature monitor cover. It was left there with me. She also strangely left a spray bottle of some sort. The other staff in the room seemed to pay no attention to her shaking and leaving things behind.

After they had left, and a guard was watching me from the other side, I retrieved the bottle. Not even knowing what it was, I soon sprayed it into my eye. It was mostly water, and I threatened to stab my eye with the thermometer cover, but I eventually gave both to the guard.

While wearing the box, I heard from demons. They showed me a wicked-looking spider that ran creepily from where I kneeled on the floor to the metal wall. I felt it telling me to write more wicked lies about higher prison staff on the wall. When I refused, it forced me, as I had no control, to drink seven gulps of water out of the toilet. Without any control, when the thought came, I just obeyed.

I was completely out of control. I then climbed up on top of the sink that was attached to the toilet and jumped. The darkness that had lived all inside of me was now all over me, no longer hiding. I belonged to Satan because I belonged to sin.

The guards rushed in, and I was still crazy, so I fought them back. When they removed me from the suicide watch room, I lashed out at the officers who were handling me and fought back, kicking and scratching, so I was given assault charges, too. The lieutenant even said that I had bitten him while being carried away. I was crazy, I was insane, I was completely mad. Having jumped, I began to bleed from the side of my left eyebrow. So, I was sent to the hospital for the second time.

As we rode to the hospital, I was convinced that I would lash out and hurt someone at the hospital. I was so afraid to go. Strangely, as the corrections officers sat with me in triage, they began to act dizzy. The older of the two, who I remembered from working often at the camp, got up and walked to the EKG machine that I was hooked up to, and he began to say that it was reading his own blood pressure.

Demonic spells that worked on me also worked on them, but theirs seemed limited and temporary. I even looked at the nurse's breasts and desired to touch them. I also wanted to compliment the buttocks of the feminine male hospital aide, but I had enough control not to do so.

Repeatedly, wicked thoughts were introduced to my mind as if giving me options. I also asked one of the officers if he would shoot me if I ran. I wanted to die but not have to hurt myself to do so. The same feminine male aide said I might need to stay three days for a urinary tract infection. Nothing made sense. Not him, not me, not anybody.

The cut near my eyebrow was not deep, but they would at least clean it. But I was afraid to be there any longer, afraid of what I might do, so I told them not to clean it and that I was ready to leave. So we did. As we left, I pretended to try to run, but I changed my mind.

Once we returned from the hospital, I went back on suicide watch for now the fourth time, where I would literally sit on the bed for hours, rocking like a lunatic and walking the floors. I would see written words on the floor and other places. My eyes even interpreted marks on my arm from the cuffs I'd worn a lot, my eyes saw those marks as "666" on my left arm. I even reopened my head stitches and wiped the blood on the walls, making short lines of blood. I even racially insulted the white male guards.

One day, while chained with the box, my eyes saw a fly that flew over to the wall, as I believed it was telling me to write something cruel about the warden. The fly just sat there until I obeyed. As I watched, I thought I was to either smash my head on the metal wall or write on it. I refused, so I then saw another tiny, wicked spider crawl quickly across the floor to the wall, indicating to me to write on the wall. So I wrote a lie with my spit that a Lieutenant was a chomo and a homo.

Around this time I went for two weeks with no bowel movement at all. Due to much lack of movement, the sour, unprocessed food would just sit in my stomach. The smell in my nostrils from my belly was horrendous. Then, they gave me magnesium citrate for the second time, and I quickly had multiple bowel movements there in suicide watch.

Around Tuesday, February 8, 2022, my case manager from the camp was the guard to watch over me for that shift. When I looked at him, I kept seeing my biological dad's face instead of seeing him. Thinking I'd soon die, I gave the case manager final words to give to my mother. I'd told him to look up my ministry on YouTube to learn that I was not always the way I had become. My mother later confirmed that he had shared with her that he had learned of my ministry online. Many prison staff do care.

Some believe that the captain is the most influential and powerful person in prison, not the warden. And that day, as my case manager watched over me, the captain came to check on me, as he had in the recent past. And this time, I told him to "F** off." The captain seemed enraged, and once he left, the case manager asked if I knew who the man was. I acknowledged that I knew, though I'd never been told. I answered: "Yes, the Captain." I steadily made more and more enemies. I even had previously told the female assistant warden: "Nice A**."

What Color Are Your Panties?

While on suicide watch, I was constantly paranoid, thinking they were putting something poisonous in the three meals they brought to me. I even believed they spat on or put the medications I often refused to take, in the food.

As the terror continued, the devil would hammer my thoughts with ideas of various things: addresses I lived at, my wife's social security number, and names of relatives. It's like I saw these and remembered what they were at first. Then, the name, number, or address would just leave my memory. And I suddenly couldn't recall what I had thought just moments ago. I'd think of relatives and cars they'd driven. I'd see their faces but could suddenly now not remember what vehicle they drove. I was obsessed with remembering what automobiles they had. I'd see other family members' faces but could not remember their names. I was sure my memory was fading away. As I tried to remember, I heard the devil say, "Blocked." I kept softly repeating my former addresses and my birthday, expecting I'd not remember them soon.

One time, when staff came in to check on me, they entered the very small, brightly lit room in a group. By then, I was no longer wearing the box; I was just wearing handcuffs and a smock. This time, a female guard recorded what was happening with a voice recorder. And right then, the devil told me to grope the breast of the female nurse. But I had the strength not to do it. So, instead, I asked her what color panties she had on. They all looked at me in disdain and disgust. Then, I got up to walk out, but the on-duty Lieutenant blocked the door. I really did believe that I could just walk out. I was demented.

Other times, I would hear the same song repeating on the radio down the hall, over and over. I was also trying to figure out if the guard could hear it too. My life was inundated with oddities and terror. Whether saying things I had no power over, hearing songs that would not stop, or forgetting random memories. I was under a spell brought on by sin and, more specifically, homosexuality.

A Fly Flew In His Mouth

Having regained some normalcy in my actions and words, I returned to wearing no cuffs. At a psychologist's recommendation, I was allowed in suicide watch to wear orange SHU clothes instead of the smock. Getting better in the mind, I even took an orange sock I'd worn and cleaned the vulgar things I had said about a lieutenant off the metal wall. It had been there for weeks. All of this proved to the psyche staff that I was improving. The chief psych even complimented me for wiping those words off the wall.

By this time, guards and upper staff would regularly ask me if I wanted to shower. I had gone weeks and weeks without a shower. Other than to wash off the pepper spray, I had not showered since being in the SHU with Tommy, who took all of the meds. I'd usually answer with a no, thinking that if they took me out of suicide watch, they'd return me to the SHU instead, so I mostly refused to shower. I hated suicide watch but hated the SHU and its noise even more. The loud shutting of metal doors and even louder inmates terrified me. So, I preferred the tiny suicide watch room over the SHU.

In the SHU and suicide watch, a toothbrush was a plastic bristle that fits on the index finger. It did not do the job. I'd brush my teeth in the SHU maybe once a week, but I would go weeks without brushing in suicide watch. To make me uncomfortable with the suicide watch room and get more out of there, I think they turned on the air conditioner. So I began to freeze there one day.

I was getting better, thankfully. But despite that, how I looked told a different story. I had initially lost much of the front of my hair, and I'd had no haircut since about November, and now it was late February. In addition, for about two months, I'd had no access to razors or nail clippers, so I looked like a horror story. I looked like the hell I had become.

A male nurse complimented me on my improvements as I continued to act more normal. By this time, nearly all higher-up staff members had stopped coming to check on me. I was even being watched over by inmates once again. One of them told me they would move me to Lexington Federal Medical Center (FMC) if I didn't get better. The lead psychologist mentioned the FMC to me, too. Further, the chief had stated, and I agreed, that it would be good to be close to home. Still, I was unsure of what would actually happen.

So, I started telling the staff what they wanted to hear because the room was cold, and I was ready to move on from that tiny space. I told them that I was no longer suicidal, and I said to them that the FMC would help me get better. But the truth is, I had no idea what awaited me.

On Tuesday, March 1, 2022, I was returned to the SHU to await transfer to somewhere other than the FCI Ashland. By this time, it seemed most of the guys I'd been in there with weeks before were gone to other destinations or back to the prison compound or to the camp. My new cellie was a guy I'd also seen at the camp. I was on the bottom bed, and he was up top, but strange encounters soon returned. After I saw a fly enter his mouth, he began to say weird things to me.

The SHU can be very boring, having nothing to do. So, he offered to play checkers with me, but I didn't remember how to play at first. We did play two or three games before I went to lie back down. He also told me that the guy who had played chess with Travis, who was actually still there, had told him that I'd been pepper sprayed. I acted ignorant of that statement. He then asked me about my plea options for my medicare fraud charges. This conversation came out of nowhere. I attempted to answer him, but suddenly, I had no idea what he and I were discussing. So, I stared absently into the upper corner wall. I knew right then that what had been with me in suicide watch was not gone. It had followed me to the SHU again. Although I did "seem" better then, I was utterly and fearfully shocked at what was happening. I was still crazy, even if I felt better.

Then, very early on Thursday, March 3, 2022, a lieutenant, the same one I had bitten according to him, came unexpectedly through the SHU hall with another officer, wanting to know which cell I was in. I still could barely sleep and would be awake all or most of the night. So, I saw and heard their conversation. I didn't know what this meant. But before breakfast was delivered that morning, I was moved to a shower to change my clothes.

A guard that many camp inmates hated, whom I had flirted with weeks prior as he watched me in the suicide watch, approached the caged shower to let me know they would be transporting me elsewhere that morning. He also warned that they would tighten the cuffs I had to wear if I gave them any problems. Clothed by this time, I had on the box while handcuffed and chains around my waist. I now had a violent record of assaulting myself and prison staff, so this was how I had to be transported - wearing a box.

From this treatment they gave me and the chains I was wearing, the Lexington FMC was nowhere on my mind. I thought we were heading to a United States Penitentiary (USP) or other higher security prison for much more hardened criminals. I'd also heard of Big Sandy, a high-security prison in Kentucky. So, I decided we were heading there. And the two guards transporting me told me nothing about where we were headed. It seemed they had prepared for a long ride with their backpacks, so I just didn't know. Incredibly out of my mind still, I just rode quietly.

CHAPTER 8
THE DEPTHS OF DESPAIR

I Had Been Admitted To The Psych Ward

I was relieved when I heard the GPS say Lexington FMC.

As we entered the city, I knew where I was—Lexington, where I was born and raised. Many of the horrifying nightmares Satan had overwhelmed me with were focused on places I lived in, Lexington or Louisville, often 1944 Chris Drive in Lexington. So, even arriving in Lexington felt like a prophecy manifested by the devil.

As we pulled up to the prison, the tall height of the gates and the ancient-looking buildings made it seem like I was entering a very dark and old era.

Having reached the processing department, I had to choose my shoe size for some shoes to change into, but I couldn't figure that out, so I got the wrong size. I just could not focus. I was then led to an office, where I lied, telling the nurse some made-up story about what my past was in Ashland at the camp and FCI as if they didn't keep tight records. There, they took a photo of me.

I was then given an ID card with the photo on it. The photograph described how far down I had spiraled, even physically. All of that facial hair, the now more empty head where hair used to be, the darkness of my eyes, and the whiskers for a mustache. This picture spoke of a man, a fallen man, who had been to hell and was still there, trapped in hell. I looked crazy at best.

The devil had told me through the book of Deuteronomy that I would see myself "mad." Now, not only did I see, but it would also become a record for others to view. The visual record of a fallen man.

I was then taken to my new living quarters, a building named "Unity." At this facility, the inmates lived in buildings that were given names.

Walking towards my living quarters, I shook uncontrollably. That March morning was cold, but this shake had nothing to do with the temperature. As I walked through the doors, I noticed that the other inmates in this unit looked normal, as I thought I looked, not actually comprehending how my face looked at the time. They all looked normal until I got to my living corridor on the first floor.

I had been admitted to the psych ward. As I walked, one guy I saw in his bed looked as though he had molested countless children. Wherever his mind was, you could tell it had been there for years, if not decades. To look at him was not to see a person but a psychologically demented man. To see him was to see something that had conquered him visibly and inwardly. Another inmate I saw, his eyes seemed to bulge open non-stop. For some reason, I got the impression that he, too, had been a predator toward children. Further, this guy's snoring was unlike anything I had heard on earth. Overall, my first impression was that I was in another world.

As I sat on my newly assigned bed, seated on a bed to my left was a man who looked full of hell and demons. He began to immediately complain and threaten me for being there. He then told the staff that brought me to that room that they had broken his teeth. Soon, the head psychologist arrived, and I looked in confusion and amazement at where I was and who my new roommates were. I then understood that it was unsafe to be in there with him. So they moved me to an adjoining room on the other side.

So, I sat in the new room assignment with nothing but the clothes on my back, trying to understand what was happening and how I had come to this place. I was shocked, I was bewildered, I was ashamed, I was embarrassed, and I was in hell still. In the bed next to me in this room was a black guy who had seemed at first to be very normal and well-kept. He looked much more normal than the others. So, I began to feel a sense of ease. But within the hour, he began talking to me about how normal he had been at the camp he had been before. He then said that a witch had been talking to him while there and that she was still talking to him there in the psych ward. This guy was normal physically, but his mind had left him, too.

I was so in shock and despair to be instantly around so many crazy people all at once. I was sure my life would never be the same.

Another guy in the room with us was "Ralph." He arrived later. He was Muslim, and when I said, "Nice to meet you," Ralph strangely replied, "Unfortunately." This same Ralph would stand in the same spot for hours and hours, just standing there. Within a day or so, I noticed feces in a used diaper on the table next to me. This diaper came from Ralph. I don't even recall being able to smell it. I didn't ask him to throw it away. It just sat there as he stood there. Was I becoming as crazy as them?

After arriving there, I realized something. When someone relocates from one prison to another, your belongings don't arrive immediately. They could take days to arrive as they are shipped through another method. So, unless you buy other clothes through the commissary, you have to wear what you have on. In some instances, you must wear prison-assigned khaki type clothes, usually worn when you leave the unit during lunch, for classes, work, and other appointments. Prison-assigned clothes frequently fit oddly, and you typically must also wear these oversized, tall black boots. So, I had to wear these seemingly enormous prison boots to dinner at this new prison compound. At the camp, we rarely had to follow these clothing rules.

I went to eat in the cafeteria for the first time. I was still not shaven, my nails not clipped, and my hair as wild as it was when much of it first fell out. But this all seemed to not matter to me at the time. As I stood in line for my food, an invisible force pushed me almost totally to the floor. This push came out of nowhere. No person stood there, but I nearly hit the floor anyway. I walked away, embarrassed, unable to explain what had just happened.

Once back in the room, I became aware that another guy in the adjoining room was just as or more insane than the others. He would roam the hallways for hours and hours at night, pacing back and forth and then into the bathroom we all shared. He would clean it repeatedly. I was startled one night as he paced the hallways and then suddenly slammed the door from the hallway to our room.

By Sunday night, I finally got a haircut from a guy who was a barber of that unit. So, some normalcy was returning.

Having arrived at this compound on the first Thursday in March 2022, by the following Tuesday, I unexpectedly learned that I could shop. Because I had been violent towards myself and other officers and been written up for it, I had lost some privileges, but I never asked which ones. I was too embarrassed at what I had become. I didn't want too much contact with staff. So, I never asked. Later, I learned I had lost the privilege of emailing people for ninety days. But I was allowed to shop with no restrictions.

So that Tuesday morning I went shopping. But something as normal as shopping was even confusing for me, and the inmates working the commissary were evidently upset with my inability to answer quickly and make simple choices. This further made me ashamed.

When I finally finished shopping and left with my large bag of things, over the intercom, I was called back to the commissary and told by two officers that I was going to the SHU. This sent me into further mental turmoil. What in the world had I done now? As a male and female officer escorted me to the SHU from the commissary, the female was making fun of how I looked in the photo they had taken of me the week before, noting how I looked different now—with a haircut. The lack of consideration and human decency from her was shocking, but I was getting used to it. Often, we are nothing to some prison staff. Just another inmate. But I also now understand that this was also more spiritual, so it likely had nothing to do with her own words, rather, the demon using her to shame me.

Once I arrived at the SHU to be processed and exchanged my badge clothes for orange ones again, the psychology staff who came there informed me that I had done nothing wrong. They informed me that I was there because I was a security risk. My mother was told the same thing, so I came to find out.

One reason you can be a security risk is if staff knows you and I learned later that at least one prison staff member there knew me. So I was again put into a cell in the SHU, now at the FMC, in Lexington.

Because of my recidivism, the points against me were already stacked. Thus, I was no longer at a "minimum" like those who were inmates at camps. I was considered a low and, in some instances, a medium risk. All of this matters even when placed in the SHU. This prison, unlike the one in Ashland, was not across the street from a camp for males, so I could easily share this cell with violent or very violent men.

I ended up locked in a cell with "Gerald," who had about 20 years left. Gerald told me that he had assaulted a woman before, so I figured that he was incarcerated for assault or maybe much worse. Prisoners don't often tell what they are incarcerated for or the entire truth. Why was he in the SHU? He was under investigation for some sort of wrongdoing he was accused of being a part of on the compound, or so he said.

Gerald seemed normal at first. We got along just fine initially. He slept on the bottom bunk, and I was on the top. He had been there before I got there. But by the second day with him, Gerald sat there suddenly acting dizzy in the chair. He quickly seemed incoherent, disconnected, and like he was changing. Something was happening to him, and all I could do was watch, not knowing what was next. This is the man I was locked in the cell with.

The SHU And Torments

In the SHU, we were allowed two ten-minute calls a month. I was so disoriented in FCI Ashland's SHU that I never used those opportunities, so my loved ones had not heard from me since late 2021.

In this particular SHU, I called my mother and my wife (now ex-wife). I called one on a weekend and another on a different weekend. When I called them, I was so out of touch with reality that I barely knew how or what to say. I felt embarrassed by the change that had taken place in me. I was sure my mother and wife could recognize it simply by my voice and my inability to be clear and concise. My wife unexpectedly asked if I had self-harmed myself. I'm unsure of my response to her.

Up until then, my mother had only been able to check on me through prison staff, such as my case manager at the camp. I could immediately tell that she was very anxious and concerned about her son. I detested calling them in the state of mind I was dealing with. Also, I didn't want them to hear me like I was. But I knew they needed an update from me directly. After these calls, I felt even worse because I was not myself.

I also avoided conversations with staff who would come through the SHU daily to check on inmates because I would forget things in conversation with some of them. So I often chose not to speak to them altogether. One staff member who walked past asked if I was still alive, maybe because I would just lay so still for hours and hours. Another one passing through insinuated that I was masturbating, though nothing I was doing gave that impression. Their statements made me more paranoid of them at the time.

Once, I actually did want to talk to my new case manager regarding when I would be designated out since I couldn't stay there. So, as he walked through the SHU one day, I called him after he passed by. We would normally not know they were coming until they passed by, and they'd often not announce themselves. When I called out, this case manager looked back and over to my cell as if he were in a daze and confused. Then, immediately, two guards angrily walked over and told me that he was already gone. Though he was standing right there near them. No matter where I went, craziness followed.

On one occasion, I was allowed to leave the cell to meet with psych staff. And just outside the cell, I saw my photo posted at the door along with my inmate number. It was the picture that they took of me when I arrived there. I was horrified just seeing it, knowing that whenever staff passed by and saw it, they would know how bad I had looked, even though I had a haircut now.

*"I Don't Give A D***"*

Odd things continued to happen. My bowels were now so negatively impacted by all of the lying around for months. When I used the bathroom, the excrement smelled more horrible than normal. What made it worse was the small space. I'd sit on the toilet for long periods, up to an hour, sitting there wishing and hoping my bowels would move. And I barely showered due to the malfunctioning showers. So, my hygiene was atrocious.

In the cell with Gerald, I experienced more of "The Twilight Zone." On one account, Gerald told me that he had counted the number of times I went to the toilet to urinate. He said I went ten times in four minutes. It was like I couldn't hold the urine, feeling like it was stinging my bladder.

I would even do things but not remember. It could suddenly become very cold in that tiny cell. One night, I filled the vent with toilet paper to stay warm. I then looked at the covered vent and could not remember having done this, though it had been moments before when I had done it. I just couldn't remember.

I would sleep for maybe twenty minutes here or there, by then refusing again to take Trazodone or Prozac. At night, Gerald would sleep violently on the plastic-covered bed below me, twisting violently back and forth. Given that I could barely sleep, whether with or without his noises, I would just lay there. To cause him to get quiet, I would make very loud snoring sounds myself. One night, while in his sleep, he began to laugh at me. These nights seemed never to end. Both day and night were tormenting.

Other times, Gerald would seemingly read my mind. I had one particularly horrible dream where I dreamt that my face had melted away. After I woke up, Gerald began to reference and talk about what I dreamed. He even once referenced a time unbeknownst to him when I had referred to myself as a Muslim when on suicide watch.

Another odd event was that demons tried to motivate me to fight Gerald, just as they desired me to do with Travis back in Ashland. However, I knew I could not whip him, so I refused the temptation to fight him. Their power over me was not as strong as before.

The nightmares soon took on a very different shape. In one dream, a white male representing Gerald went mad and overpowered my stepfather and brother and then came after me. This dream occurred at an apartment we used to live in when I was in elementary school. While this was only a dream, upon waking, Gerald soon paced the floor for hours for days in a row, claiming he was working out. But Gerald was changing.

The times that we used to get along seemed to become less and less as the days went by. He was more annoyed and irritated with me, much more. He would look at me and flex his muscles in front of me. This began to frighten me. He would even get close to me, and I would ask, "What are you doing?" He would reply, "You know." I was terrified of him, so to calm myself, I would softly sing a song I made up, softly singing repeatedly: "There will be no fight."

By then, I slept for about one to two hours, normally during the night. And when I did sleep, I had so many dreams of people forgetting me. I even dreamt that Jade, my beloved daughter, had forgotten me. I dreamed about a stadium filling up for a fight and another of me in a prison yard being flirted with by many men. I additionally periodically saw gnats that would appear out of nowhere and soon disappear. They would bounce on the walls as if telling me to run my head into the walls. I was even given a vision of myself, old and maniacal, and locked in a steel-walled prison room all alone. This horrified me so very much. I believed that the devil owned my future. He wanted me to think that life as I knew it was over and that the devil did own me. But the truth was, the day would break. It was already breaking, and deliverance was nearing. But not quite yet.

I began to learn that these demons did not have control of me like they had before. Their grip over me had loosened, and their hold over me subsided. So, they wanted to use Gerald since they couldn't use me.

It was now Tuesday, March 29, 2022. I had been locked in a cell with Gerald for about three weeks. Like the previous Tuesday, Gerald wanted my bed made. As usual, the warden and other staff would come through the SHU to see how we were doing. It was said that inmates may get in trouble if the beds were not made. I didn't follow his wishes the week prior, and I was determined to leave the bed as is.

Just like the dreams I'd been having for many days, Gerald suddenly became violently hostile and extremely enraged towards me. In turn, I told him he did not tell me what to do. So, he

137

responded by saying that the warden ran the prison, and that he (Gerald) ran that room. He had also made some racist-related comments to me days before, so this may very well have played a part in him feeling disrespected by a black man. Either way, he was full of rage and abruptly walked to the metal door.

It was then that one of my dreams of him began to manifest. Gerald hit the cell heavy metal door with such force, grunting with hot anger and indignance, that the guy across the hall, having heard it, rushed to his own door to see what was happening. It was with such force that I literally thought the door might break. So I hurried to get up and I began to make the bed. My heart was pounding as I hurried to obey Gerald. He did eventually calm down. But for GOD, I was sure he was going to kill me. I became afraid that he was a bomb waiting to go off. Tick tock...

I waited until later that night when he was asleep. And I secretly passed a note to a passing guard. The guards would do rounds and check on us all day and night. I wrote a note with a bendable plastic-type pencil, which was the only writing utensil allowed in the SHU. The note said that Gerald had threatened me and that my life was in danger. I saw the guard read it, and I also saw him never return to rescue me later on that night.

The next day, I prepared another note, and when Gerald was not paying attention, I gave it to a different guard. When they came around to provide us with clean linens. I then proceeded to ask the guard if he read it, and he replied, "I don't give a d***." It was apparent to me then that I had lost all control of the situation I was in. I worked hard, reminding myself day and night that there would be no fight between him and me.

Thankfully, several days later, when Gerald had gone out to the small yard for recreation time for residents of the SHU, instead of bringing him back to our cell, they put him somewhere else. Maybe my note made a difference after all. Or maybe he complained about how bad I smelled. I'm unsure. But I was very glad to be free of him.

I Was In A Hole, And I Could Find No Way Out

I was then alone, but not for long. "Tim," who apparently had deep mental issues, was my new cellie. Tim slept a lot, maybe due to meds. When people can't fix you, they often load you with medications.

Late one night, I observed him walking the floors, even into and out of the shower. He was not a maniac like Gerald, but he was still obviously toiling in his mind. When I woke up and noticed this odd behavior, he stopped to go back to bed.

It was around this time that I again started taking Trazodone, the meds prescribed to me back in Ashland. Though I had chosen not to take them, they were still available to help me sleep and for depression. But I still refused the Prozac.

While in the cell with Tim, I was told I had a legal call and was then escorted out to a lieutenant's office, the designated place to take such calls at this prison compound. My court representative for the divorce, "Mr. Matthews" wanted to speak with me on a call. The lieutenant looked at me with disgust as I had to use his phone and office. This was also maybe due to how I looked with

139

no haircut, having been in the SHU for weeks, and the odor of my often unwashed body. I felt like trash in front of this very uncompassionate lieutenant. To him, I felt I wasn't a person, just an inmate.

I became more confused when I got on the phone with Mr. Matthews, so much so that he asked if I was in prison for drugs. I sounded different to my wife, my mother, and now to this stranger I had never spoken to. I could barely even answer his questions. What had happened to me impacted me on so many levels. Psychologically, I was someone else, literally.

The call was to see if I contested the divorce, and ultimately, I did not. But I could not answer simple questions and I felt foggy in my thoughts, possibly due to the Trazodone. I felt so ashamed that I had fallen so far in my mind. I felt completely worthless to everyone. I was in a hole and could not find a way out. So I steadily accepted this new me, this new look, this new Dominique.

Taking Trazodone nightly did help me start to sleep, maybe not for very long, but for longer than I had been. So, I kept accepting it when the nurse came by nightly with the meds that inmates were prescribed.

Even with Trazodone, falling asleep would still take me an hour or more before sleep took over. What made matters worse was that Tim left, maybe after about a week of being my cellie, and "Mitchell" moved in. Mitchell's snoring was tremendously loud during the time before I would fall asleep. Snoring in such a tight space sounds even louder than normal. His snoring was a complete distraction to me. So, to help calm myself down due to his loud snoring, I would holler "sleeeeeeep" repeatedly for hours. But he slept through it. I later discovered that the people next door, through the vents, could hear me hollering. I did this many nights until breakfast showed up, which would be around 6 am. So, when the meds could help me sleep, I was often kept awake due to his noises. In the morning, I would thank GOD I had made it through another night of loud distractions.

During a phone conversation with my wife, I apologized to LaShonda for all the wrongs I did while married to her. I did not seek to regain her love. I was past that. I just wanted to apologize.

My daughter's birthday was approaching on April 11th. So, in April, I wrote Jade a letter. I was very embarrassed that it was written so poorly with that plastic pencil, but I was determined to let her hear from me for her birthday. It was her Sweet 16. I pushed myself to write to her, trying to do something familiar to me, to celebrate her life.

I also began to try to reach out to GOD again. I asked the chaplain, who regularly visited the SHU, for a Bible and one of those Daily Bread monthly pamphlets. I began reading both. It had dawned on me that my only hope was GOD. As sick as I had been and become, I was now well enough to know that I could be saved from all of this.

So, I began to find hope. But it seemed as though I progressed from terror to despair. When I met with my case manager for a routine visit, he also provided me with documents about my recidivism, which is related to an inmate reoffending. Further, it can also include new violations, and I indeed had several. Given the transition I had been in from one location to another, I had no written documents to confirm what trouble I had gotten into until now.

At the camp in September 2020, I had a very low 5 points because I was there for a white-collar crime. I was considered a minimum. But by this time, between the self-harm violations and assaulting two officers, I had 24 points, 23 of which were violent. It was hard for me to even wrap my mind around that. I looked at the pages my case manager left with me in the SHU with utter disbelief. My prison record was equal to actually being violent. I tried to ignore this, but paperwork and surely violations follow you, in prison (they really do).

Eventually, Mitchell was released from the SHU, and my case manager told me I was designated, but he would not tell me the location. In the meantime, I got a new cellie for a few days. He seemed very psychologically disturbed. Early on, he told me that he missed his mind. It was a reminder to me that my mind was gone. That cellie was gone on or around April 20, 2022, and I was alone.

CHAPTER 9
THE BEGINNING OF REDEMPTION

I Began To Cry

A day later, I was on a plane heading to Atlanta to pick up other inmates. When being moved from one location to another in prison, one normally travels by plane or bus, depending on the distance.

During this plane trip, I was very withdrawn, as this was the first time since the camp that I had been around so many people all at once. And it humiliated me all the more to be wearing handcuffs on a plane and in public.

After leaving Atlanta, we flew to Tulsa, Oklahoma. During the flight, some guys who sat with me on the way to Tulsa said that they were heading to some psych program in Indiana. They both seemed very mentally out of touch, so I concluded that I was going there with them. But the Tulsa facility they were transferring us to was a holding spot for inmates transferring from one prison to another. I was not told how long I'd be there.

Further, due to my recent violent history, there I was separated from the general population and put in the SHU again.

All of the unknown that surrounded me kept me horrified. Not knowing what existed in my near or distant future made me very uncomfortable and restless.

When they finally told me where I was going, they said I was going to Milan. One female staff member said she didn't know what level it was. But a male guard said that it was a medium. They had to both have known. This was torture to hear. I turned from them and began to cry.

The FCI Ashland was a 'low,' and Lexington's FMC was technically a 'low' too. However, because it was a sort of hospital as well, I believe it housed inmates with minimum, low, medium, and I expect higher security levels. So, to understand I had been so very violent that I was being transferred to a medium, it boggled my mind and confounded and overwhelmed me. I silently wept and cried. So there I was, in the SHU, once again, in Tulsa, Oklahoma.

That same day, a new cellie came in. He was a very handsome, light brown-skinned man heading to a medium in Texas. He kept telling me how bad the food was at the USP (U.S. Penitentiary). All I could think of was how terrible food would be when I got to where I was going. He then quickly ate the food they brought us as if he hadn't eaten such a good meal in years.

I continued to take Trazodone, so it helped me get sleep. On Friday, April 22, 2022, as he rested on the top bunk, he looked down at me and made a flirtatious comment. The expression on his face was one of lust. Suddenly, I remembered the kinds of sexual acts that got me there in the first place. But still, I chose it again that day. We were intimate with one another. It happened so very quickly. One moment, he was staring at me, and the very next, we were being sexual with each other. We eventually relieved our own selves.

It happened again the following day. Afterward, I asked GOD to forgive me. I also told my cellie we could not do that again. He consented to my decision. He said it would be our secret. However, as usual, once this was over, I still felt empty.

Sex with the same sex never actually satisfies, ever. There is nothing permanently fulfilling about homosexual acts, nothing. To think there is any fulfillment is to be deceived.

In the early morning of Monday, April 25, 2022, he left the SHU to head to his next destination, and sometime later that morning, I was on a plane heading to Milan.

This trip was different from the one to Tulsa. Due to my recent history, I was put in the same type of box I wore during the trip to Lexington's FMC. I suspect this was to protect myself and others from me. Of the hundreds on the plane, only a very few wore a box. Just like the previous time in suicide watch, I had added chains wrapped around my waist and regular handcuffs on as well. This was a tighter fit and more painful than wearing regular cuffs.

I was so very embarrassed, attempting to hide the box under my white T-shirt on the plane. Looking down as we flew, I saw a familiar football field in Ohio, so I was sure we were heading to

Michigan, though I didn't yet know Milan was in Michigan. Some other inmates in transit told me that Milan was actually a Low FCI. So I knew I had been lied to by the guard in Oklahoma. I was content, at least, to be heading to familiar territory, as I had lived in Michigan from 1999 to 2010. After arriving in Michigan at a small airport, I was soon put on a bus heading to Milan, MI, to the Low FCI.

It Was Time For Some Mass Deliverance

The handcuffs and box came off later that Monday, April 25, 2022. That would be the last time I'd ever wear handcuffs again.

I was processed into the prison there in Milan. I was interviewed by both my case manager and a female psychologist. The stack of pages the case manager had for me was huge. I tried to read some of what was written. From what I could catch, some of it appeared to be warnings about how I acted in the past and what they may expect from me. I suppose that is why a psychologist met with me as well. She asked me if I had sexually assaulted an inmate, I guess referring to the PREA, and I said no because that never happened.

I then went to the unit, where I would be quarantined due to COVID-19. Unlike the fall of 2020, quarantine was some, maybe sixty of us, on a second floor together. We could move around the floor all together. But this was not the general population; this was the SHU, too. We just didn't have the cell doors locked; we were free in there together. And we had no guards constantly watching over us.

A tall black guy, "Jeff," who was there for drug criminal activity, was my new cellie. Jeff would sometimes say weird things to me. Also, there was another guy, "Ronald." Very early on, Ronald threatened me, like Gerald, that previous cellie, about cleaning the cell, even though he was not my cellmate. But he soon became nice to me over time.

My experience in Milan was initially slightly similar to what had happened in Lexington and Ashland, but not nearly the same. Some days later, I moved to the empty cell across the hall from Jeff because I wanted my own space. I was happy to be alone. These cells were older and much more dilapidated than the newer SHU in Lexington.

I was still taking Trazodone, so my sleep continued to improve. However, the enemy still minorly interacted with me through others, not just Jeff and Ronald. The male nurse who would give me my meds in the late afternoons there in the SHU-style quarantine cells seemed very angry when handing them to me.

Quarantine was good for me there in Milan. I was isolated most of the time for those months, so quarantining with about sixty guys before going to the general population of about two thousand was needed. This was like baby steps, which was good because I began interacting with other inmates. I would play card games and have conversations. I would read books, go to the TV room, and read The Daily Bread, a Christian devotional book often distributed to churches, prisons, and homeless shelters. I even began taking regular showers and working out again. I began to feel somewhat normal again, both mentally and physically. But I still looked like hell. Jeff had told me how my eyes looked like raccoon eyes, and Ronald had told me how dark I looked. I may have made it out, but "it" had not made it out of me. However, an incredible breakthrough in restoration was only days away.

In quarantine, I was allowed regular phone calls. Due to COVID, we still had 510 free calling minutes a month. So, I began making calls. I called my wife and mother, but I also called some of my siblings and some spiritual family. Every one of these calls began to deliver me, as the people who had no idea what had happened to me began to pray, to talk, and continue to pray, and to minister me out of my trauma and what all I had endured. One of my biological sisters, Sharnita, had told me on one call that week: "Let the devil hear your roar, GOD..." I knew this meant that GOD was using her to serve notice to the devil that the hold he had on me was coming to an end. And that the devil who had been roaring in my head and life *(1 Peter 5:8)* for many months was now about to hear GOD roar back at him. The Lion of the Tribe of Judah *(Revelation 5:5)* was about to roar back!

To GOD be The Glory because every call I made brought about a reversal. The enemy was losing his grip even more.

On Friday, April 29, 2022, I called my best friend of many years, Prophet Michael Holts. We first became friends as we played church outside together as children decades before while living in the same apartment complex. During this call, Prophet Holts reminded me that I must confess my sins in order to be forgiven. So, I did just that on Saturday, April 30, 2022. I got on a call with my spiritual parents, Bishop Michael, and First Lady Stacey Densmore, and I confessed. I shared about the homosexual life

I had lived and, more specifically, the sin I had committed with the guy in the shower in the fall of the prior year in Ashland.

Restoration began with this call.

James 5:16 (KJV)

"Confess your faults one to another, and pray for one another, that you may be healed (restored)"

GOD had begun rebuking the enemy from me mightily, but now it was time for some mass deliverance.

I Got The Holy Ghost Again!

After revealing and explaining my sins to my leaders, the next day, Sunday, May 1, 2022, I called my mother, Betty Jones, and my stepdad, Marcus Jones—who is very actually much a father to me. Both of them are called to ministry. At this time, they were on a trip in Cincinnati. During that call, my father quoted the scripture:

2 Timothy 1:12 (KJV)

"...For I know whom I have believed, and am persuaded that He is able to keep that which I have committed unto Him against that day."

I immediately understood that GOD was telling me that He now forgave me for my past sins. And that because of the confession I made the day before, those sins no longer belonged to me but were now nailed on Calvary's cross, buried with Christ.

I experienced true repentance and forgiveness. Reflecting on that time and thinking about GOD's Word, I experienced the following scriptures:

149

- *I John 1:19 (KJV):* *"If we confess our sins, He is faithful to forgive us our sins and to cleanse us from all unrighteousness."*

- *Psalms 103:12 (KJV):* *"As far as the east is from the west, so far hath he removed our transgressions from us."*

- *Acts 3:19 (KJV):* *"Repent ye therefore, and be converted, that your sins may be blotted out…"*

Now, my past faults belonged to Him. Then my father, Elder Marcus Jones, began ministering to me about being refilled with The Holy Ghost according to *Acts 2: 1-4*:

1 And when the day of Pentecost was fully come, they were all with one accord in one place.

2 And suddenly there came a sound from heaven as of a rushing mighty wind, and it filled all the house where they were sitting.

3 And there appeared unto them cloven tongues like as of fire, and it sat upon each of them.

4 And they were all filled with the Holy Ghost, and began to speak with other tongues, as the Spirit gave them utterance.

So, that is precisely what started to happen.

I went back to the cell, and I began to sing the song written by Elbernita (Twinkie) Clark and later sung by the late Reverend James Moore: "Endow Me." In that cell, I sang: "Endow me, with the power of The Holy Ghost." Before I knew it, as I sang the song, I began to vomit into the toilet there in the cell. It happened so suddenly and without warning or expectation. Having experienced deliverance before, I knew exactly what was occurring, though I was still stunned. I regurgitated things, spiritual things that had been locked inside of me. I regurgitated them right there into the toilet. I was so thankful to see this happening, finally. GOD was answering the prayers of all of those calls I had made. He was delivering me. And He was about to endow me after He began to clean me inwardly.

A little later that same evening, I was on a call with a spiritual son of mine, Prophet Seneca of Illinois. He met me through social media seven years prior and joined the ministry of The Ecclesia of Prophets, which I formed in 2017. He led and taught them while I was away in federal prison. On that call, he began ministering and talking about "restoration oil." As Prophet Seneca told me to lift my hands, I soon started to weep and cry. But before he said it, my hands were already raised, and I was even on my knees in the hall as others saw and passed by. However, I did not care what they thought. I had not spoken in tongues since at least 2021. But there on that floor, GOD began to re-baptize me. GOD was coming back inside of me! I was thrilled! I was excited! I was ecstatic! I was humbled! I was overwhelmed with joy! I was on cloud eleven! The nightmare had ended, and I was finally waking up! Again, I spoke in tongues as The Spirit of GOD gave utterance *(Acts 2:4)*.

No More Mental, No More Trazodone

By Monday, May 2, 2022, things began to change rapidly for me. As I reached out to GOD, He began to pull me out of the remaining mental bondage.

151

Though I had been consistently taking Trazodone since early April, still my sleep was often unusual, at best. Yes, I could sleep, but it would sometimes take a while for me to fall asleep, and taking that medication made me so unfocused at times. So much so that I could be even more susceptible to demons while on the Trazodone, I soon learned. But I kept taking it every evening after the nurse gave them to me.

On Tuesday, May 3, 2022, Ronald, who had told me how dark I looked just a few days ago, now told me how much brighter I looked. Jeff, who'd just told me I had raccoon eyes days before, now began telling me my eyes looked better. What was happening on the inside was manifesting on the outside!

By this time, I began working out more and more. In the quarantine, we didn't have free weights to use, so I would lift laundry bags with books inside of them. And I began to put on weight. During those months of demon possession, I figured my weight had dropped to about 130 lbs., but now I was around 145 lbs. I was getting my strength back, both spiritually and naturally. The prophecy of natural and supernatural strength was prayed over me just days ago by a spiritual mother to me, Prophetess Addie of New York, who is also a member of The Ecclesia.

From December 2021 to that moment, my bowel movements were tremendously unbalanced. However, having been restored and beginning to be refilled with The Spirit of The Holy Ghost, I began having regular bathroom breaks without fiber pills, magnesia milk, or magnesium citrate.

While still in quarantine, on Saturday, May 7, 2022, I had a standard meeting with my case manager. At this time, he told me that I qualified for the First Step Act (FSA). A law was put into place in December 2018 to allow inmates to get up to an entire year off of their sentence if they met certain qualifications and criteria.

On Tuesday, May 10, 2022, I gladly, though skeptically, moved from quarantine to Unit B2, an open dorm on the prison compound. It was somewhat similar to the camp dorm, though much older, not nearly as clean-looking, and very dilapidated. At this time, I began having daily interactions with many people as I moved throughout the unit and compound.

Over the next few months, periodically, an inmate would make a strange statement to me, which I could tell was inspired by the devil, but those were seldom and dwindling.

On Friday, May 13, I had access to a scale and was happy to see that I now weighed 154 lbs. While most of it was not muscle, I was glad to be in a body I recognized more.

On Thursday, May 26, 2022, I called my daughter Jade. We had not talked since the fall of 2021, when I had soon thereafter begun to have a very nervous breakdown. She loved talking to her dad, and I surely loved speaking to her.

I began to feel whole again. Family is also wholeness.

By early June, I continued to take Trazodone only 1-3 times a week, typically only on the weekends. I did this to get even more prolonged sleep then. But I took it less and less because it left me groggy and somewhat disconnected, even after I'd had much sleep, well into the next day.

During these heavily induced sleeping nights, I would sometimes fight in my sleep, I was told by my new cellie and other inmates. Once, I nearly fell out of bed. It was becoming clear that the Trazodone opened passageways where the enemy could be more involved with me when I slept.

At this time, I was also making more calls to family and friends, describing to them in detail what had all happened to me. They were overjoyed to hear that I had made it through.

Then, on Wednesday, June 22, 2022, it was confirmed that the psychology board of this prison had moved me from a mental care level 3 to a 2. In Ashland, it had been raised to a 3. The highest was a 4.

On Wednesday, June 29, 2022, I met with my psychologist at Milan FCI, other prison staff, including the chaplain, and the head psychologist of the compound. They asked me questions, and I updated them on how I was doing psychologically and on my prison activities. They could easily tell I was not what the documents said I had been just two months ago. A change had happened.

Then, on a call on Friday, July 1, 2022, LaShonda informed me that our 23-year marriage was dissolved. The divorce was now finalized. When the possibility of divorce was initially told to me, it helped make me insane. It devastated me and ultimately helped cause traumatization. But now it was okay for me to hear. I was not happy that she divorced me. I was unhappy being single, but

I was at peace with it. GOD was healing me. And I wanted to live.

On Tuesday, July 5, I weighed 161 lbs, and on Wednesday, July 20, 2022, the psych dept downgraded me from a mental care level 2 to a mental care level 1. According to the psych doctor, all of the inmates on the compound, though mostly all normal, were on a mental care level 1. I no longer had to have meetings with her. It sure felt good to be normal again and thought of as normal. However, I was still taking the prescribed high Trazodone dosage.

So many good things were falling into place for me. And I even began taking a small business class weekly as I also spent much time writing the book you now read.

On Friday, July 22, around 1:30 am, having taken 100 mg of Trazodone, I had a night of terrors, much worse than previous drug-induced nights. The following day, others who had noticed it commented to me on it. So, on Saturday, July 23, I decided to flush the remaining Trazodone down the toilet, and I never retrieved them from the nurses again. They clearly helped to make me very vulnerable and susceptible to demon powers when I slept. What man chooses to fix us with may actually be a door for the devil.

Fresh Oil, Even In Prison

During that same month, other Christian brothers and I started praying in one of the unit stairwells each night. It felt good to find and connect with other Christian men in prison. Some nights, there would be ten or more of us praying together.

On Monday, July 25, more manifested purging and deliverance occurred in me. These 'purgings' would happen unexpectedly, in the shower or the bed, manifesting by unprovoked belching, vomiting, and yawning out of nowhere. The closer I got to GOD, the more demons left me. Yes, I had received The Holy Ghost again, but I was now daily being filled.

The more He fills you, the more the devil has to go. They can't continue to live where GOD lives.

In August, some brothers and I began holding weekly services in the chapel, which later moved to another room. Within weeks, the small room was packed. This ministry was called Fresh Oil Prison Ministries. Various nationalities would attend, no matter what their background or crime, they would come and be welcomed. A man named James and I would lead it, and the power of GOD would fall tremendously as men wept, repented, and turned back to GOD.

At this time, GOD began telling me more and more that I'd soon be released. By November, I learned that my FSA had finally kicked in. Inmates had heard about the FSA at the camp, but it was now implemented, and qualifying inmates' sentences began to have their sentencing terms reduced. Inmates were immediately released, and others were soon released to go home. This began happening nationally by the thousands.

My sentence and good time credit had reduced my release date from Friday, September 12, 2025, to Thursday, March 7, 2024. Due to good behavior and other factors, I would spend about 7 months in a halfway house or on house arrest until the March 7th date, when the sentence would finally end.

It's concerning that I could hurt myself while on suicide watch and be written up for it. This and fighting back at the prison staff caused me to lose a lot of good credit time. Months of good credit, actually. I later tried to argue this time loss and the added recidivism points. But it fell on deaf ears. However, GOD has the final say and is in complete control everywhere and at all times.

Thinking back, LaShonda's prophecy had come to pass. She had told me in early 2021 that if I were not careful of various conversations, it would extend my prison sentence. After I conversed again, through calls and emails with the Maryland professional, I found that when I did this, it led to other doorways. My world, mind, emotions, and actions flipped upside down. I chose not to listen, and my sentence was extended by months due to lost good credit time.

When a true prophet has prophesied to you, listen, and keep listening, and obeying.

Getting Free From Drunkenness And Drunk Men

When Jesus/Yeshua sometimes performed miracles and delivered people, it would sometimes be read that it occurred that same hour *(Luke 7:21)*. Yet, for many, deliverance is not immediate. That hour may mean the same week, the same month, the same year, or even longer.

By early 2023, GOD allowed me to notice signs, mostly when lying down to rest or sleep. At times, these signs would manifest, letting me know that the enemy was still inside of me somewhere. It was made known to me by a movement in my body that was not made by me. A twitch, or motion not initiated by me. I became aware that this was GOD telling me that He was not done cleaning me of what unholy things had come into me. I battled with this because I just felt like I should be completely clean by now.

To explain this, GOD transported me by vision to approximately 2015. He transported me to a time when I had been making out with a young man in a shopping center parking garage. When I saw this reminder, I further realized I had let devils in me for decades. I understood that back in 2015 and even 2005, and way before then, I had opened doors that devils had entered into me. While they were not permitted to possess me anymore, by the summer of 2023, some still lived in me, somewhere they did.

Some of us are, even to this day, oppressed and affected by demons, which can easily manifest in our bodies through various illnesses, both physical, mental, and emotional. That is why I was still being processed through deliverance for many months. My "hour" was actually many months.

Oppression is a door to possible possession. Definitionally, oppression is a burden, an imposition, or restraint. It is harsh, something heavy lying upon another, and it weighs down. Oppression has the power to subdue or weigh down and make one weary. It presses upon and against its subject.

Sin causes mankind to enter the process of oppression by devils and demons, and that individual then has less and less health, less and less peace, less victory, and more defeat. We will realize this is true if we pay attention. Devils seek ownership, to possess us, to have entire control. He wants to own our lives, so much so to where we have no peace mentally or health physically. He seeks to possess, to own. He seeks possession.

I had chosen for decades to keep giving my will to my own desires. So then, eventually, the devil did not want to have partial or temporary control over me.

When we sin, we open doors, and devils and demons often come through those doors, taking up residence and space inside us. This is a fact founded on scripture, for when Jesus/Yeshua cast demons out of people, He would often finish by saying, "Go and sin no more" *(John 8:11)*.

Sin is the doorway for devils into our bodies and lives. That is why some people can't stop lying, can't stop cheating, can't stop stealing, can't stop masturbating, being bitter, being negative, cursing, getting high, getting drunk, and so on. The more you can't stop, the more it's possessing you or beginning to possess you.

Depending on the extent and length of our unclean life, our "same hour" may be the "same month." It could also take a day or a few minutes. How quickly or slowly it happens depends on how soon and how much we detach from evil and then allow GOD to fill us through our relationship with Him.

Renouncing and denouncing involvement with devils and their attached sins are essential to successful deliverance. **Matthew 16:19b** informs us that *"…whatsoever thou shalt bind on earth shall be bound in heaven: and whatsoever thou shalt loose on earth shall be loosed in heaven."* We can't bind what we are still bound/tied to. It will not work.

The speedier we discontinue wrongdoing, the quicker we will obtain and maintain deliverance. If we want deliverance from sin, any sin, anything that The Bible calls sin, then we must be willing to let it go. We can no longer be bound to it, holding on to it, being one with it, not if we truly desire deliverance from its authority over our lives.

Also, necessary is further explained in **Ephesians 5:18-21**:

18 And be not drunk with wine, wherein is excess; but be filled with the Spirit;

19 Speaking to yourselves in psalms and hymns and spiritual songs, singing and making melody in your heart to the Lord;

20 Giving thanks always for all things unto GOD and the Father in the name of our Lord Jesus Christ;

21 Submitting yourselves one to another in the fear of GOD.

These verses teach what one must do to become filled with GOD. We want sin and can become obsessed with sin because of our focus on doing wrong. Continuing to do wrong allows us to possibly become oppressed and possessed by its demons. Since we're not filled with GOD, we become filled with the devil. The wine in verse 18 can also be whatever we get drunk with. We can drink and become drunk with wrong relationships, drunk with being envious, critical, argumentative, combative, hateful, resentful, and unable to forgive. Further, we can be drunk with pain pills, cigarettes, vapes, and marijuana, and the list goes on and on. It can also mean being drunk with literal wine or alcohol. So, verse 18 teaches us not to let anything own us. In other words, to not be drunk with it. It owns you and possesses you when you become intoxicated with it. When it overwhelmingly affects your speech, movements, thoughts, actions, and reactions. This is when you've moved from sinning and into oppression and then into a time when it starts to possess you.

Further, verse 19 tells us how to be filled with Him, how to allow His Spirit to come into us, and how to get drunk with GOD. He does not only want to fill the space around you, the church you attend, or the room or vehicle in which you play Gospel or Christian music. But He wants to literally fill you. He wants to fill you. Not just to the point that your language changes, which we already learned in *Acts 2:1-4*, but He wants to fill you daily and without limits.

Daily fillings easily happen through what we say, and hear from others. Is it possible to pray to and praise GOD every minute of 24 hours a day? No. But for GOD to have no part in most conversations in your daily life is only going to lead to sin. Why? Because prayer gives us discernment and direction. Choosing not to pray means you don't really know who is around you. You think you do, but prayer reveals the truth.

Watch what you say and pay attention to what others are saying to you. Then, decide if it adds to your values, or your flesh, to your sin, to your desire to do wrong. Decide if it subtracts from your own relationship with GOD. Sin is often introduced through acquaintances and conversations.

Just as you have people you work with, people you get your hair done with, people you talk to on certain occasions, you ought also to have, every day in your life, those who play spiritual roles in your life. People who advance your spiritual growth and development. People you can easily have GODly conversations with and talk to about GOD, scriptures, and the love of GOD. What you say and hear from others will play a massive role in what role GOD plays in your life.

Being 'surrounded' may not be in person. It can be in your text messages or inbox. In the past, I chose to surround myself with people who wanted the lust, perversion, and sins I longed to satisfy daily. And often, one comment or picture received or video sent to them had me somewhere soon pleasuring myself. What was on and in them got onto and inside of me.

The supreme purpose of those previous relationships in my life was to hold me back, to hinder me. To cause oppression and, eventually, possession. They were there to keep me from progressing in GOD and to keep me holding onto sin. I became one with countless males. I was bound and emotionally tied to countless men. If you want deliverance from sins and their devils, pay attention to who you fellowship with, who you walk with, and those who are a regular part of your day.

Ephesians 5, verses 19 and 20 also tell us that if GOD is going to replace what we have been drinking and possibly become drunk with, then we must engage Him through singing, praising, thanksgiving, and worshiping—by making melody and music in our hearts and with our open mouths unto The Lord.

Yes, we drank the pleasures of sin. Whatever those sins were, we drank them.

Somebody reading this, maybe you got as drunk as me. Maybe you get so drunk that it took over you like it took over me. Or maybe your drunkenness led to losing your child or children like I lost my daughter's relationship for years. But there is an exit ramp, a detour, and a way out. Not only must you reconsider who you walk and talk with, but you must boost, prioritize, and strengthen your walk with GOD. Get drunk with the presence of GOD and with The Word of GOD. Fill your space and time with GOD!

As sins and demons are leaving us, they will only remain absent from us as we seek to fill the space where they once lived. It is important to drive the devil out and to also fill the space they once lived in.

Matthew 12:43-45 (KJV)

[43] *When the unclean spirit is gone out of a man, he walketh through dry places, seeking rest, and findeth none.*

[44] *Then he saith, I will return into my house from whence I came out; and when he is come, he findeth it empty, swept, and garnished.*

[45] *Then goeth he, and taketh with himself seven other spirits more wicked than himself, and they enter in and dwell there: and the last state of that man is worse than the first. Even so shall it be also unto this wicked generation.*

In these New Testament verses, Jesus teaches us that once a devil is cast out, it searches and looks for what is dry, empty, and where nothing else lives. This spirit, this unclean spirit, could only find rest in emptiness and where it was waterless. But verse 43 says he found no rest. Also, this demon refers to the house it left as still his. The devil we once served will always believe he owns us. So, it's up to us to change his preconceived ideas.

The devil returns to his old habitation, though the house was swept, cleaned, and put in order. This demon/sin that the homeowner/me/you got drunk on in times past, this same demon then recruits seven demons more wicked than himself, ensuring it won't be quickly evicted again. They move into the empty and dry house, the scripture says. And the end result of that man, the homeowner, is worse than before, the scripture says. It's not good enough to be delivered of the devil, demons, and sin. Rather, it is just as essential to be filled and to remain filled with GOD.

CHAPTER 10
THE FINAL SURRENDER

Letting GOD Free Me

As deliverance continued inside of me, so did the legal process of the FSA, which allowed me to get out of prison in advance.

By January 2023, I knew that I could easily walk into my case manager's office and have him register me to leave in March so I could spend up to 12 months at a halfway house or on home confinement. Typically, case managers and other prison administrative staff are much too busy to call you into their office for such. It's normally up to inmates to initiate this process. So, I was eager to see my case manager, as I noticed others going home on the FSA.

Despite my eagerness, GOD spoke to me and reminded me of two scriptural passages: the story of Paul and Silas *(Acts 16: 16-40)* and Joseph's prison experience *(Genesis Chapters 39-41)*. Even after their cuffs and bands were loosed, Paul and Silas remained imprisoned because the mission was not yet accomplished. Also, GOD reminded me that just as Joseph used his gifts in prison and ministered to other inmates, He informed me that I was to continue to do the same. So, I was led by The Lord to not interfere with any attempt to speed up my release date. GOD wanted me to continue to focus on ministry there. So, instead of quickly initiating release from prison, I continued to lead Fresh Oil Prison Ministries.

Every Saturday, I was in service, and GOD continued to pour out His anointing as men wept before The Lord and turned back to Him. I also continued to lead the stairwell prayer group, even though some of them had gone home already.

I waited from January through April 2023. I did not interfere, I did not interrupt, and I did not engage in the release process. I was committed to allowing GOD to do this on His time clock. Obedience is better than sacrifice *(1 Samuel 15:22)*.

When a new case manager took over my case in April, he called me in to start relocating me to return to Kentucky. Because my case originated in Michigan, first, they had to confirm that I had somewhere to go and live in Lexington, Kentucky, which would be processed through a probation office. I already knew that this process could take weeks, if not months, and that I could have started this particular process many months ago. This step had to be done before registering for early release.

The relocation process was initiated on Friday, April 21, 2023, instead of during 2022. Obedience is better, and GOD's timing is always best.

While the process seemed to prolong, it was all the divine timing of The Lord. After a probation officer visited my parents, where I would temporarily live, an unexpected delay seemed to lengthen the process even more. So, I became angry with GOD and the fact that I chose to obey. I thought, why couldn't He do His job and hurry up? Then, in a vision, The Lord showed me a snail. A snail that moves slowly at its own pace. As I looked at the snail, I noticed its long antennas and immediately understood that if a process is delayed, it is only because GOD can see what's ahead. I also understood that my future outside of prison was not ready for my arrival. I concluded that this delay had a purpose and that GOD could see much further than I could. So peace settled over me as He got me out, not myself.

Once the relocation process was completed, I was officially put in for release to the halfway house. I was put in around early July. But even that is a process that must be signed off by prison staff, even more so because of the record I had obtained through various actions while incarcerated. Meanwhile, James, who had helped me to start and lead Fresh Oil in prison, had already gone home, so I was now leading the ministry with Van and Nicholas, who I recruited to take over after I was gone.

By then, Fresh Oil services were in a larger room on Saturday afternoons, and the crowd continued to grow. GOD continued to move and ignite repentance. I worked with Van and Nick to prepare them to lead in my absence. The service grew numerically, and so did the two of them.

Finally, on Thursday, July 20, 2023, approximately one week after my case manager submitted my name for release to the halfway house, I was informed by the case manager that I would leave FCI Milan and head to the halfway house on Wednesday, August 16, 2023. Joy and happiness filled me! In less than a month, I would be free of imprisonment! A five-year sentence had suddenly become less than three years! What was slowed down was suddenly speeding up! It came quickly!

On that same day, I was fingerprinted, as is protocol when an inmate is in the process of leaving prison. A prison secretary began to initiate my furlough and the itinerary for my release date. I would be traveling by bus back to Kentucky, so all of this had to be organized by the prison in less than 30 days!

I had about three weeks to finish pouring into the men at our services. I began teaching lessons on holiness and leprosy, how leprosy can be equated to one's sin and iniquity, and how sin brought us all to Milan FCI. We were not in Milan just to serve time. We were there to become clean of sin, repent of our wrongdoings, and return to GOD.

For some, repentance can mean sooner release. But whatever it means, at the least, it ought to mean that we leave our passions for sin and come back to GOD and a holy lifestyle. And a holy life does not mean boring or lacking excitement and enjoyment. GOD wants us to be happy! But it does mean not doing what displeases GOD!

That's Not You!

As I prepared to be released to my childhood home of Lexington, I was about 170 lbs and muscular, and I continued to lift weights five days a week. The physical me going home was different from me on Monday, September 14, 2020. I also spent time with people like "Rick," a married man with two sons who had gotten in trouble and was given a 46-month sentence. He had only been there for about four months by then.

Rick was a regular attendee of our Fresh Oil services, and he lived in my unit, so I would periodically sit, talk, and minister to him. During one conversation with Rick, I showed him my inmate ID, which was issued to me on Monday, April 25, 2022, when I arrived at Milan FCI. Amazingly, while looking at the photo, Rick explained what he saw in the 'Dominique' in the picture taken of me, compared to the man who now sat next to him.

Definitionally, leprosy is a chronic (prolonged and lingering) disease causing ulcers (an inflamed lesion on the skin) and sores on the body. Spiritually, it is an infection that enters the soul and lifestyle through actions and deeds that we commit. Leprosy can even enter through things we say, sexual acts, and so forth.

Sin can introduce the soul and life to famine and barrenness—maybe my sins brought forth LaShonda's two miscarriages. Sin can bring financial ruin, mental health issues, physical ailments, actual diseases, and so forth. Sin and its devils are never satisfied. They will always want to conquer and to control.

John 10:10 (KJV)

"The thief cometh not, but for to steal, and to kill, and to destroy: I am come that they might have life, and that they might have it more abundantly."

This verse clearly states the intention of the enemy. He comes to kill, steal, and destroy. As mentioned in a previous chapter of this book, the devil believes he owns us. He had decided such the moment that we gave in to him and that he entered our lives. Deciding that we now belong to him, he also has decided that he will not just steal from us and utterly kill us, but on the way to that death, that he will destroy us. For me, this included the horrifying things I said and did, especially in the SHU and suicide watch. It was intended to produce destruction.

Destruction: The devil wants to tear us apart, tear apart relatives from one another, husbands from wives, tear our minds apart, tear us from our health and peace of mind. Tear the man from knowing he is a man and the woman into engaging sexually with the same sex. To make it more personal: The devil is determined to steal from you, to kill you, and to destroy you. Make no mistake about it. This is his endgame, and he will not stop until he completes his assignment or at least tries his hardest.

In that same verse, Jesus/Yeshua said, *"I am come that you might have life and that more abundantly."* For every plan from the devil, there is a plan from GOD. As is stated in **Genesis 50:20**, after Joseph had gone from apparent familial stability and a good life, he ended up in a pit and then in prison. In verse 20, we understand what the devil meant for evil; GOD turned it around for Joseph's good.

The devil was committed to keeping me in prison. That is why he wanted me to touch the nurse's breasts, and why he had told me to stab the doctor. He was committed to his scenario for me and, at the very least, to keep me completely crazy and mentally deranged. But in prison, I found life, and that more abundantly. What the devil intended to keep me bound with, fettered forever and hooked on prescription meds and entirely out of control, but

170

GOD turned it! He had another plan! He rescued me! He rescued me! He rescued me!

You're not just reading a book. This is a prophecy: GOD is rescuing you and your children. He's rescuing you into your future! The way it is - is not the way it will stay. It's all shifting, it's turning, it's reversing, it's becoming better. A total shift is happening in your favor! This is The Word of The Lord! This is The Word of The Lord!

The entire time I was away from freedom, GOD was setting me free from leprosy, from sins, and from iniquities that had belonged to me for decades.

No matter how long we have sinned. It does not have to continue in our lives. The devil will try his best to give you his end, his death, to kill you. But Christ Jesus has come that you may have life and that more abundantly! Let life begin! Let His will for you start!

Matthew 4:4 (KJV)

"Man shall not live by bread alone, but by every Word that proceeds out of the mouth of GOD."

What I had been eating, drinking, and consuming for decades. The places I'd frequented, the men I slept with, the seeds that became my deeds and habits, all of the pornography I watched and masturbated to. All of these constantly fed my own will, my desires, my own needs, my lusts and carnal longings. The more a man or woman eats and drinks, the more they can eat their way into obesity and even morbid obesity. So much so that where

171

what they consume can eventually, in turn, consume and kill them.

There is, however, another option. Man shall not live by bread alone! Jesus came that we may have life and that more abundantly. His Word, The Holy Bible, and a relationship with Jesus feeds our spirit man, our inward man. Where the flesh misled you and me, GOD seeks to return us to Him. The more we drink, eat, and consume GOD, the more our mind leads us to GOD and away from our desires.

I didn't eat His Word much for years, mainly only to minister to other people. Consequently, my soul was in danger, and eventually, I fell into a horrifying pit. That fall which progressed for years resulted in spiritual ulcers and sores, crabs, chlamydia, intensified anxiety and worry, sleeplessness, raccoon-like eyes, extreme thinness, cussing people out, and darkness all over my countenance. My mind was ripped to shreds. My body and soul were darkened because my flesh had led the way. Flesh led by sin and sin introduced to me by demons.

3 John 1:2 (Amplified Bible)

"Beloved, I pray that in every way you may succeed and prosper and be in good health (physically), just as (I know) your soul prospers (spiritually)."

My soul followed my flesh, sin, and its demons, so I crashed. If you want to be rescued and freed, you must be willing to put what you wish aside and accept the plan of GOD for your life.

In the summer of 2023, when Rick looked at that April 2022 photo of me, he said he saw a picture of a "bruised, beaten, destroyed, defeated" Dominique. He said I had raccoon eyes in that photo, and that my cheekbones and face had fallen and sunken. But then he said, "You (now) look fair and brighter." He said: "That's not you." He could now see that life and that life more abundantly. Rick said that had he not heard from me that it was me in that picture, he'd have said: "That's not you."

Regeneration is real. Restoration is real. More than that, GOD is real!!!

Cursing Out The Chaplain And Bowing Before Satan

On Wednesday, August 16, 2023, I left the Milan FCI prison and boarded a Greyhound bus to return to Lexington, Kentucky. The last time I was there was when I was incarcerated in early March of the prior year at the FMC. But this time, I was going home in my right mind. My end-of-sentence date was still Tuesday, March 7, 2024, and I expected to be at the halfway house for maybe a few weeks and then on to home confinement with my parents there in Lexington.

Though due to additional expectations to move to Louisville over the next several months, which were my plans, my stay at the halfway house, until my sentence ended, seemed very likely as March 7th approached.

While at the halfway house, I didn't feel tempted by homosexuality for months, and then it started. As I continued to work on this first book of mine that you are reading, I realized that every desire I stayed free from was not completely gone. There was still a desire inside of me to return to the deeds that had collapsed me.

Over the weeks and months, I began to learn to follow, pray, and then accept what Jesus prayed and accepted. In **Luke 22:41-42**, Jesus was given an option. He could either accept the will of GOD, or His own will. He could choose to accept the cross of Calvary, or He could choose the will of the man inside of Him and live and not be killed while all of us perished.

A combination of scriptures teaches that Jesus was all GOD and all Man. While we all should seek and receive the free gift of The Holy Ghost as described in **Acts 2:1-4**, the fact also is this: GOD breathed into us; it was part of Him, His breath, we call it spirit. **Genesis 2:7** teaches that GOD breathed into Adam's nostrils. This spirit/breath is called the breath of life in verse 7. Spirit is life, and life is spirit.

When GOD/spirit/life entered Adam, he became a living soul, says verse 7. This spirit that comes from GOD goes inside the man, bringing the man to produce a soul. The soul is sometimes called the inward man. It is the free will of man. It is the part of us that can make choices, so it is likened to the mind. The soul is also the immaterial essence of a human being that gives them individuality and humanity.

The soul/mind is the part GOD gives us that can decide whether to lead us to GOD or not. I can choose GOD, if I choose to. GOD/breath/spirit breathed into Adam and into you, then we became souls. The soul, thoughts, and mind can lead us to a fulfilled and obedient walk with GOD, or not.

In *Luke 22:41-42*, Jesus prayed: *"Not my will…"* In other words, Jesus was saying, I don't always want the will of GOD for me, but I will submit to GOD's will anyway. If Jesus felt this way, surely we will at times, too. So every single day, like everyone else, who has a sinful present and or past. You and I have the option to choose His will. In *Joshua 24:15*, the successor to Moses, Joshua, tells Israel to make a choice. To choose who they will serve. He called on them to make a decision.

You don't have to be forced to sin. I became forced/possessed when I violently crashed my head into that sharp metal corner on Tuesday, December 28, 2021. I was still possessed later when I opened the stitches and put the warm blood on the suicide watch walls in early 2022. And soon after that, I cursed GOD because I was possessed and I was forced. I was also forced in early 2022 to curse out the chaplain in front of a psychologist and then get on my knees and bow down, worshiping the devil in front of them both. But that's no longer me. And it does not have to be you.

This book is a turnaround in your life.

You Need The Holy Ghost

I was not always forced. You are reading this book because you're being given a chance. An opportunity and a choice. Prayer, worship, and praise to GOD, reading The Bible, and a daily relationship with GOD will all aid you in doing His will, as it does me. But not only these, you also need the infilling of The Holy Spirit/Ghost. We learned in *Matthew 12:43-45* that the devil who left this man sought dry places. Dry means lacking moisture. This means where no water is, it is waterless and dry.

In verses like *Isaiah 44:3*, *John 4:13-14*, and *John 7:37-39*, we realize that biblically water refers to His Spirit. When you receive the free gift of The Holy Spirit, as stated in *Acts 2:1-4*, this is His Spirit, His River coming inside of us.

The demon in *Matthew 12* was searching, but everywhere he looked, it said he had seen no dry place. Dry places are the only ones where He was able to find rest. Here's the revelation - where he did look, he saw water; he saw The Holy Spirit. So, he could not rest or find a home there.

Where GOD fully is, Satan cannot live. This demon that was searching could not live where GOD filled the space. You must not only let GOD in you, you must allow His Holy Spirit to fill you. Otherwise, it's possible for the enemy to take us space, which is what happened to me the more I sinned.

You don't just need to pray and talk to GOD. Ask GOD to fill you with Himself. Ask for The Holy Spirit/Ghost. I began to be filled again on Sunday, May 1, 2022, and now is your opportunity.

Perhaps you never struggled like me with your sexual identity, but please don't fool yourself. You struggle right now, whether you see it as something small or something significant. We all struggle with something or another. Be honest with yourself. You do have struggles.

And whatever your struggle is, whether nicotine or unforgiveness, or gambling, you can be free.

Romans 12:2 (KJV)

"And be not conformed to this world: but be ye transformed by the renewing of your mind, that you may prove what is that good, and acceptable, and perfect, will of GOD."

The soul is linked to the mind; some say they are one. When your mind is changed, you change. And there is no better antidote and cure for the will of man, and the mind of man, than the mind of GOD. And what is the mind of GOD? What are the thoughts of GOD? The Bible, The Word of GOD. The Word of GOD is the mind of GOD.

Philippians 2:5 (KJV)

"Let this mind be in you which was also in Christ Jesus"

When your mind changes, you change. When my mind changes, I change. We may never fully hate what we learned to long and lust for. But the power given to us through a relationship with GOD, His Word, and the Holy Ghost will help us avoid things we learned to desire with our flesh.

Romans 7:19-25 (KJV), Apostle Paul wrote:

19 For the good that I would I do not: but the evil which I would not, that I do.

20 Now if I do that I would not, it is no more I that do it, but sin that dwelleth in me.

21 I find then a law, that, when I would do good, evil is present with me.

22 For I delight in the law of GOD after the inward man.

177

²³ But I see another law in my members, warring against the law of my mind, and bringing me into captivity to the law of sin which is in my members.

²⁴ O wretched man that I am! Who shall deliver me from the body of this death?

²⁵ I thank GOD through Jesus Christ our Lord. So then with the mind I myself serve the Law of GOD, but with the flesh the law of sin.

Paul, who is responsible for writing a vast majority of books in the New Testament, is human, just like you and just like me. And he is teaching us how to become free. He makes it plain that even though he wants to do what is right, he isn't. He says he is failing in his walk with GOD because of his flesh. This honest apostle is telling the truth and speaking very candidly about himself. This gifted man admits that he is in error. That evil is what he is doing, and that he is not walking righteously. But he does not leave us or himself without any hope.

This is the same Paul who has the The Holy Spirit, but is still a man nonetheless. He admits to a powerful struggle. As he writes, he causes us to realize that sin dwells in himself. And because of that sin, evil is winning. The sin lives in his flesh. The skin we were born in is dedicated to getting us in trouble. Our flesh is solidly determined to lead us to hell.

Paul is saying in verse 21 that he wants to do good, but evil, no matter how far he runs to GOD, evil is still present. The flesh is still with him, he says. I can't get away from it, he says. I was born with it, and I'll die with it. When I wake up, it clings to me. When I open up my mouth, its lips are moving. When I walk, it wants to lead my path. Because it's forever attached to me in every way.

178

It wants to govern my senses. Looking in the mirror, I see it looking back at me. It seems I can do nothing without it. The flesh. Always present.

Verse 22 also confesses that something else inside Paul and us wants to serve GOD. The Amplified Bible says that this is our new nature, the converted me. But there is still a struggle. Paul continues on saying in verse 23 that there is another law, rule, and action living inside of himself. He's making it known that for all of us, there is a will to do good, and a will to do wrong.

Apostle Paul confesses for himself and for us all that we are all wretched. No matter how good we think we have become. No matter how talented, gifted, and saved we think we are. Every one of us is one choice, one decision, one wrong move, from causing chaos in our lives. It can all happen with one wrong decision.

So, Paul then asks in verse 24, Who will deliver/rescue/free us from the direction we're heading in?

Then he gives us all a solution. It is a very simple and easy solution to a life that can quickly become chaotic and complex. He says that if I do what my flesh, desires, and appetites want, it will only lead to sin and ultimately spiritual death *(Romans 6:23)*. But he goes on to say that his mind is able to serve GOD. The mind can choose. The mind can change. A renewed mind has the complete capability to shift our whole life.

If we can adopt Christ's mind, every challenge we face will be won, every struggle broken, and every habit abolished.

Everything that seeks to oppress and possess us will lose its power and grip and no longer control us or our future.

If you still think it's impossible to change, think again. Paul also said, *"I can do all things through Christ, who strengthens me"* **(Philippians 4:13)**.

The positive decisions you begin making after reading this book will absolutely and radically change and uplift your entire life.

Renouncing, Denouncing, And Confessing

Romans 10:10b (KJV)

"…with the mouth confession is made unto salvation (deliverance)."

This scripture tells us that we can be delivered through what we say.

Mark 11:23b (KJV)

(You) "….shall have whatsoever (you) say."

Open your mouth and repeat with me this prayer and confession:

> Father GOD, in the name of Jesus, I thank You for bringing me to realize where I fall short in my life, where I fail You, and where I need to be corrected. And thank You that I was never alone. Whether right or wrong, You never left me. You were and will always be here for me **(Hebrews 13:5)**. And because You are with me now. I do have the power to positively change, shift, and uplift my life and entire future.

I embrace this moment and I move forward. I repent of everything I've done and every door I opened through sinful actions—actions that helped to shape my life into an unGODly individual and in a direction that displeased You and Your Holy Bible.

I testify, proclaim, and confess on this day that the wrong choices I've made and the wrong relationships I have been in no longer control my life. I now renounce and denounce and separate myself from anything and everybody that is not holy, in Jesus' name.

From today on, and moving forward, The Relationship that will add goodness, peace, joy, and righteousness to my life is a relationship with You. I commit to allowing You to consistently help me each day until I am no longer who and what I was.

I belong to You, GOD. I don't belong to my past, my mistakes, who I slept with that I was not married to, and the soul ties that I knowingly and unknowingly agreed to. I belong to You. I belong to You. My mind, will, and soul, from this day forward, are going to daily yield to do what You will. And anything, spirit, or demon that I accepted into my soul, body, and life through homosexuality, lesbianism, or any other form of disobedience, I cast it out and away, now, In Jesus Yeshua's Name!

I belong to You, and today is a new day. This moment is a new day. Now is a new day.

I will no longer be conformed to this world; be one with this world and its superficial values and customs. But I will be transformed and progressively changed as I mature spiritually, by the renewing of my mind *(Romans 12:1-2)*. I will daily focus on GOD values, ethical attitudes, and pure ways. A consistent relationship with You through Bible study, prayer, and worship of GOD will help this to happen. I also ask that You fill me with The Holy Spirit according to *Acts 2:1-4*.

I belong to you, and today is a new day. This moment is a new day. Now is a new day.

In Jesus Almighty Name.

All of this that I said is so and all done now.

In Jesus Yeshua's Almighty Name.

ABOUT THE AUTHOR

Dominique Trumbo is a dedicated father to his daughter, Jade Trumbo, and a seasoned prophet with nearly 30 years of experience. After graduating from high school, he pursued studies in computer science before embarking on a lifelong journey in ministry. His prophetic calling has taken him across the United States, where he has ministered under the prophet's mantle, reaching countless lives through outreach efforts, television, radio ministries, church speaking engagements, and a large social media presence.

From 2001 to 2015, Dominique pastored churches in Michigan and Virginia, leading congregations with a heart for service and spiritual growth. His work in ministry has been recognized and supported by respected leaders, including his ordination by Apostle Tudor Bismark and Bishop Iona Locke.

Dominique networked with and provided leadership to ministries in India, Pakistan, and Germany. He also founded and began to lead a school of prophets in 2017, which still thrives till this day.

In addition to his ministry, Dominique founded and managed a successful marketing and consulting company in the healthcare sector that employed approximately forty people across several states.

This book marks his debut as an author, and he intends to continue writing for the glory of GOD, with the hope of bringing salvation and inspiration to people around the world.

Dominique Trumbo

I would love for you to stay connected with me as I continue my journey of ministry and writing. Follow, engage, and keep in touch through the following platforms:

Website: Visit my official website for updates on upcoming books, events, and more:

www.DominiqueTrumbo.com

Email: For personal inquiries, prayer requests, or ministry updates, reach out via email:

info@DominiqueTrumbo.com

Social Media: Connect with me on social media for daily inspiration, insights, and up-coming events:

- **Facebook:** Dominique Trumbo II
- **Instagram:** @prophetdtrumbo
- **Threads:** @prophetdtrumbo
- **Tiktok:** @dominique.trumbo
- **YouTube:** @Prophet_D_Trumbo

THANK YOU FOR READING!

I hope this book has blessed you, inspired you, and impacted your life. Your feedback is incredibly important, and I'd love to hear from you!

Leave a Review and 5-Star Rating

How to Leave a Review on Amazon

1. Go to the book's page on **Amazon** (search for the title or author).

2. Scroll down to the **Customer Reviews** section.

3. Click on **"Write a Customer Review."**

4. Select the number of stars and write your feedback.

5. Click **Submit**—and that's it!

Thank you for your support. Your feedback can help others find this book and experience the same life-changing message. May GOD continue to bless and guide you on your journey.

Made in the USA
Columbia, SC
12 November 2024

8ee022c6-7a2e-46ad-a12c-9253ab87782dR01